SPECTRUM

Writing

Grade 4

Published by
Frank Schaffer Publications®

Lauren Barton

Frank Schaffer Publications®

Spectrum is an imprint of Frank Schaffer Publications.

Send all inquiries to:
Frank Schaffer Publications
8720 Orion Place
Columbus, Ohio 43240-2111

Spectrum Writing—grade 4

ISBN 0-7696-5284-0

4 5 6 7 8 HPS 11 10 09 08

Table of Contents Grade 4

Chapter 1

Lesson 1 Group Words and Ideas

NAME _Lauren_

A truck has just delivered boxes full of these items to your hardware store. Now, you must take each box to the correct section of the store. Decide whether each box goes to the garden section, tools section, or electrical section. Write the names of the items under the correct headings.

Garden	Tools	Electrical
Shovel	Saw	Switch
Seeds	hammer	Cord
Soil	Pliers	Lamp
Plant	Screwdriver	lightBulb

Lesson 1 Group Words and Ideas

Grouping things is a good way to organize. Lynn needs to organize these items so that she can begin to clean up her room. Think of three categories into which the items fit. Then, write the categories as headings and list each item under the correct heading.

3 dirty socks a set of magnets a photo album	1 dirty pair of jeans 4 books 1 shirt with a spot on it	2 horse figurines a box of modeling clay a journal

Heading: Dirty stuff	Heading:	Heading:
3 dirty socks 1 dirty pair of jeans 1 shirt with a spot on it		

On Your Own

You can make a game out of groups and categories. Write some categories on slips of paper. Here are some ideas to get you started: Blue Things, Things that Buzz, Things with Zippers, Fruits, Fluffy Things, Scratchy Things, and so on. One player draws a category. Then, everyone has one minute to write down as many things as they can think of that fit the category. After one minute, everyone shares what he or she wrote. All players vote on whether to accept answers that seem to "stretch" the category.

Lesson 2 Find the Main Idea

What is this picture about? Underline the sentence below that tells what the whole picture is about.

Everyone is unhappy.

The teacher does not know what to do.

This year's play is "Little Red Riding Hood." √

The sentence that tells what the picture is all about is the **main idea**.

Here is another picture. Underline the main idea of the picture.

Bill wore his brown coat today.

Bill fell on an icy patch. √

Winter is Bill's favorite season.

Lesson 2 Find the Main Idea

Look at this picture. Write a sentence that tells the main idea.

Main idea: _____

When looking at a picture, look at everything that is happening and then decide what the whole thing is about. The same thing can be done with a paragraph. Paragraphs have main ideas, too. When reading a paragraph, think about everything that is happening and decide what the whole thing is about.

Read this paragraph. Then, underline the sentence that tells the main idea.

> Kira mounded up the mashed potatoes on her plate until they looked like a volcano. Then, she pushed her peas in a ring around the base of the volcano. As she poured gravy over the peak of the volcano, she pretended that lava was flowing toward the village.

Kira played with her food. ✓

Kira likes mashed potatoes.

Kira put on too much gravy.

NAME _____

Lesson 2 Find the Main Idea

Read the paragraph and underline the main idea below.

> When we think of volcanoes, we usually think of a cone-shaped mountain with a hole at the top. Many volcanoes do look like that, but there are also many that do not. Some volcanoes are rounded at the top and have vents, or holes, on their sides from which lava flows. One volcano started out simply as a hole in a field.

A volcano is a cone-shaped mountain with a hole at the top.

Rounded volcanoes have vents on their sides.

Volcanoes come in different shapes.

Now, write your own paragraph. Write about your favorite season of the year. When you are done writing, read your paragraph. Make sure that it is all about the main idea.

Main idea: _____ is my favorite season.

_____

_____

_____

_____

_____

_____

_____

_____

Lesson 3 Find the Details

Now, take a closer look at this picture.

Details are the little parts that make up the whole picture, or main idea. For example, one detail is that the woodsman is carrying an ax.

Write two more details.

Detail: _____

Detail: _____

In a picture, many details make up the whole picture. In a paragraph, details tell about, or support, the main idea. Read this short paragraph. Identify one detail and write it below the paragraph.

> The annual fourth-grade play was especially successful this year. The student actors loved the play and really put their hearts into it. In addition, the musical talents of Miss Winslow, the student teacher, added to the performance.

Detail: _____

Lesson 3 Find the Details

Read each paragraph below. For each paragraph, identify two details and write them on the line provided.

The humane society needs volunteers. The staff is trained to care for sick animals and to interview people who want to adopt animals. There are many other tasks, however, that volunteers can perform. The animals must be fed and exercised daily, of course. Cages and walkways need cleaning as well. Finally, someone is needed to answer questions from people who are visiting or choosing a pet.

Detail: _____

Detail: _____

Volunteer opportunities in our community are endless. The senior center is always looking for people to write letters, read out loud, or visit with residents. The elementary school needs "reading buddies" to read once a week with first- or second-graders. The high school needs math and science tutors. The humane society needs help with feeding and exercising dogs.

Detail: _____

Detail: _____

Write a paragraph about a person at your school. It might be a teacher or a student, the principal, or a classroom helper. Use details that tell about the person to support your main idea. When you are finished writing, underline some details in your paragraph.

_____

_____

_____

_____

Lesson 4   What Is a Topic Sentence?

The main idea of a paragraph is often stated right in the paragraph. The sentence is called the **topic sentence**. The topic sentence and the main idea are really the same thing.

Read this paragraph. Think about what the main idea is.

> I never dreamed that the beach would be so great. We had perfect weather. The beach was clean, and the sand was so fine that it sifted through our fingers. We built a huge sand castle and decorated it with shells and driftwood. I'll remember that day forever.

Now that you've read the paragraph and thought about the main idea, underline the topic sentence. Remember, the topic sentence states the main idea.

The topic sentence is often at the beginning of a paragraph. Sometimes, though, it might be in the middle of a paragraph or even at the very end. Here is an example of a paragraph in which the topic sentence is not at the beginning. After you read the paragraph, underline the topic sentence.

> I watched the gray sky come lower and lower. I felt as if I could reach out and touch it. If I did that, though, I would get soaked. It seemed like the rain would never stop. I hate rainy days.

Lesson 4 | What Is a Topic Sentence?

Find and underline the topic sentence in each paragraph. Remember, the topic sentence might be at the beginning, in the middle, or at the end.

There is always a first rain, in April or so, when in the space of one day, the world becomes green and lively again with each droplet. As the roots come alive, leaflets stretch upward from their long sleep. A spring rain is a marvelous thing.

All rain is not the same. Some rain brings a gentle mist that dampens the world but does little more than that. Other rain brings a soaking, even drenching, wetness that affects everything. The lawn squishes under your feet, and even a raincoat doesn't keep you dry. Finally, there are the real rainstorms when you stay indoors and watch. Only the boldest or unluckiest people go out, dashing to cars or into houses.

Now, write your own paragraph about rain or a rainy day. When you are finished writing, underline your topic sentence.

_____

_____

_____

_____

_____

_____

_____

_____

Lesson 5 Stay on Topic

Most of the details in this picture fit the main idea, but one does not. Describe the detail that does not fit.

_____

Now, write a sentence that states the main idea of the picture. Ignore the detail that does not fit.

_____

Normally, all of the details in a picture fit the main idea. The same should be true of a paragraph. Each detail should fit the main idea. This means that each sentence must stay on topic.

Here is a good paragraph. It starts out with a topic sentence. Then, each sentence gives details about, or supports, the topic sentence.

> Silent reading time is my favorite time of day. It happens every day after lunch. When we come into the classroom, we all get our books out. Then, each of us goes to a reading spot. We can read anywhere in the room as long as we're not in someone else's spot. I like to curl up next to the window. For the next 25 minutes, I can go to the moon, India, or wherever my book takes me. That is why I like silent reading time.

Lesson 5 Stay on Topic

Read each paragraph. Underline the topic sentence. List two details that support the topic sentence. Then, draw a line through the sentence that does not support the topic sentence.

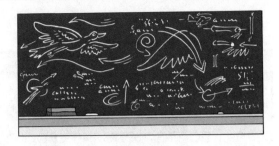

Mr. Hansen always starts the day with a joke. I don't know how he comes up with a new one every day, but he does. In class, he explains things so that we understand them. Sometimes, that means he explains them more than once. Once, he completely covered the chalkboard with drawings to help us understand how a bird can fly. Birds have hollow bones. It wasn't even science class, but we learned a lot. Mr. Hansen is my favorite teacher of all time.

Detail: _____

Detail: _____

The time line that goes around our classroom helps us keep historical events in order. In the back corner, there is a picture of a pyramid. In the next corner, there is a picture of Roman soldiers. They carried long spears and wore helmets. In the third corner, an English castle is taped to the wall. In the last corner, there is a photograph of the Wright Brothers' airplane. Finish the circle around the room, and there is our class picture.

Detail: _____

Detail: _____

Lesson 6 Write a Paragraph

Here is what you know about paragraphs.

- A paragraph is a group of sentences that are about the same topic.

- Each sentence in a paragraph expresses a complete thought. Each sentence tells about, or supports, the paragraph's topic. In other words, each sentence stays on topic.

- The main idea of a paragraph is what the paragraph is about.

- A paragraph's main idea is usually stated in a topic sentence. The topic sentence can be anywhere in the paragraph.

- The first line of a paragraph is indented.

The paragraph below has several problems. Write what the problems are below the paragraph.

Deep in a large, circular mound of earth, a scientist finds a pearl necklace. A few feet later, he finds a blade made of a hard, black stone called *obsidian*. These and many other objects help us learn about the Hopewell culture. Between 100 B.C. and A.D. 500, the Hopewell built round and octagonal mounds. They did not ride bikes. Some surrounded by miles of earthen walls. Based on what they left behind, we know that the Hopewell were an organized people with artistic skills.

Problem 1: _____

Problem 2: _____

Problem 3: _____

Lesson 6 Write a Paragraph

Imagine that you are a scientist or historian who has just found an amazing object. It might be a dinosaur bone or a gold coin, a jeweled bracelet or a stone tool. Write a paragraph about the object or about finding the object. If you wish, you may make up information about where the object came from.

_____

_____

_____

_____

_____

_____

_____

_____

_____

_____

_____

_____

_____

Questions to Ask About a Paragraph

Does the topic sentence express the main idea?
Does each sentence support the topic sentence?
Does each sentence express a complete thought?
Is the first line indented?

Chapter 2
Lesson 1 Why Do We Write?

In general, there are four purposes for writing:

- to entertain
- to persuade
- to explain
- to inform

Writers use many forms of writing, such as friendly letters, reports, news articles, book reviews, and poems. Here are the purposes for writing, along with the forms of writing that writers usually use.

Purpose for Writing	Forms of Writing
To entertain	stories, poems, plays, personal accounts or narratives, humorous articles, friendly letters
To persuade	letters to the editor, business letters
To explain	how-to instructions
To inform	reports, news articles, book reviews, personal accounts, friendly or business letters

Writers may combine purposes in one form of writing. For example, a writer may both entertain and inform in a news article about hedgehogs.

Here are some writing assignments that Mrs. May's students have completed this year. Write what you think the purpose of each assignment was—to entertain, persuade, explain, or inform.

Assignment   **Purpose for Writing**

a letter to the editor about school uniforms   _____

a story with talking animals   _____

an article about a class project   _____

instructions for using the class computers   _____

Lesson 2 For Whom Do We Write?

When a band performs a concert, an audience listens. The band director chooses music that the audience will enjoy. For example, the band would not play very serious music for an audience full of children or "Twinkle, Twinkle, Little Star" for a group of grandparents.

When a writer writes, an audience reads. A writer needs to think just like a band director does.

> What will my audience enjoy?
> What are they interested in?
> What will make them want to keep on reading (or listening)?
> What will they understand?

Listed below are some possible audiences. What might they be interested in reading about? Choose topics from the box and match them up with a possible audience. Some topics might match with more than one audience.

Writing Topics	
your last soccer game	a book report
a report on school lunches	an account of a field trip
instructions for a computer game	

friend or classmate: _____

parent: _____

grandparent: _____

teacher: _____

principal: _____

Lesson 3 Make an Announcement

Your school is holding a special event for all students and their families. The event is called *Reading Counts!* In addition to a book sale, there will be reading activities and games with free books as prizes. Your class has been asked to help out.

Your first task is to make some posters for the school hallways. The posters should get the other students interested in the event. What might the poster say that will make students want to attend? Remember to make up a date, time, and location for the event. Draw a sketch of your poster here.

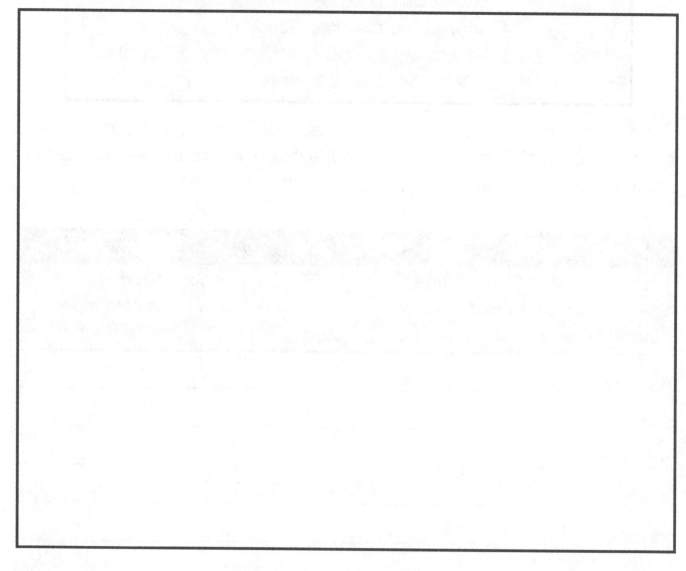

Lesson 3 Make an Announcement

Your second task is to create an announcement about the event that will be sent to all parents. What information will parents need to know? What will make them want to attend the event? Make up details as needed to persuade your audience to attend. Create your announcement here.

Now, compare the poster and the announcement. What information did you include on both items? What information did you include on one but not the other? Why?

_____

_____

_____

_____

Lesson 4 Write a Friendly Letter

A friendly letter is one that is written to someone known. A friendly letter might share family news, cheer someone up, or thank someone for a gift. Here is a friendly letter that Ned wrote to his cousin.

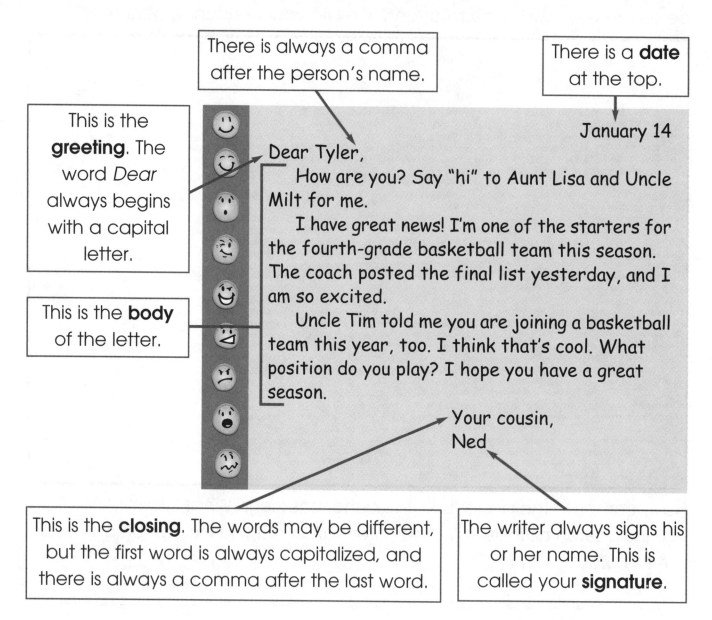

There is always a comma after the person's name.

There is a **date** at the top.

This is the **greeting**. The word *Dear* always begins with a capital letter.

This is the **body** of the letter.

January 14

Dear Tyler,

How are you? Say "hi" to Aunt Lisa and Uncle Milt for me.

I have great news! I'm one of the starters for the fourth-grade basketball team this season. The coach posted the final list yesterday, and I am so excited.

Uncle Tim told me you are joining a basketball team this year, too. I think that's cool. What position do you play? I hope you have a great season.

Your cousin,
Ned

This is the **closing**. The words may be different, but the first word is always capitalized, and there is always a comma after the last word.

The writer always signs his or her name. This is called your **signature**.

Lesson 4 Write a Friendly Letter

Ned wrote his letter because he had some good news to tell. He knew that his cousin Tyler would be interested because Tim plays basketball, too. So, Ned was keeping his audience in mind.

Now, write your own friendly letter. Write to someone who has similar interests, or who will be interested in some news you have. Look back at the letter on page 22 and follow the format for a friendly letter.

Lesson 5 Write Instructions

What if you had to explain to someone how to play a game, make a craft project, or brush your teeth? Would you be able to do it?

Lena has written instructions about how to wash dishes. She is hoping her younger sister can read the instructions and start helping!

     First, close the drain and run warm water. Put two squirts of dishwashing soap into the sink. When the water in the sink is about as deep as the length of your pointer finger, turn it off. Place each item into the water and rub it with the dishrag until it is clean. Then, rinse the item under hot water and place it in the drying rack. Always wash the dishes in this order: glasses, silverware, plates and bowls, serving dishes, and finally pots and pans. When all the dishes are washed, let out the water and rinse the sink. Finally, rinse and wring out the dishrag and hang it under the sink.

Lena did a good job with her instructions. She used **time-order words**, such as *first*, *then*, and *finally*, to make the order of the steps clear. She also used good descriptions. Phrases such as "two squirts of dishwashing soap" and "as deep as the length of your pointer finger" make her instructions very clear.

What do you think you could explain clearly in a paragraph? Write a few ideas here.

_____   _____

_____   _____

_____   _____

_____   _____

Lesson 5 Write Instructions

Look back at the your ideas on page 24. Choose one and write some brief notes about the basic steps. Write as many steps as you need.

Step 1: _____

Step 2: _____

Step 3: _____

Step 4: _____

Step 5: _____

Now, write your instructions. Remember to use time-order words to help keep everything clear. Refer to your notes as needed.

_____

_____

_____

_____

_____

_____

_____

_____

Questions to Ask About Instructions

Do the instructions include all of the steps in the correct order?
Do time-order words make the order of steps clear?
Do good descriptive words help your readers know just what you mean?

Lesson 6 Sell It!

Print advertisements are all around us. We see them on T-shirts, in magazines, and on book jackets. We see them on benches, buses, billboards, and ball caps. They are everywhere!

A good print advertisement is easy to remember. Some have a great picture or image that sticks in your mind. Some rely on strong words. Many combine images and words to communicate their message. However, all advertisements have one goal and that is to persuade.

Think of a product for which you would like to create a print ad. It might be a product you use, or you can make up a new product. Then, answer these questions to help you plan your print advertisement.

What is the product? _____

Who will use or buy your product? In other words, who is your audience?

_____

Where would be the best place for your audience to see this ad? Think about the product as well as the audience. For example, if you are advertising a computer game, which would be a better magazine to advertise in, *Outdoor Living* or *Gaming Galore*? If you are advertising a skateboard, think about where skateboarders go and what they do. Advertisements on park benches, hats, T-shirts, or in a magazine on skateboarding are effective. List as many as you think would be appropriate for your product.

_____   _____

_____   _____

_____   _____

_____   _____

Lesson 6 Sell It!

Writers who create advertisements probably pay more attention to their audience than any other type of writer does. If a writer tries to sell a product to the wrong audience, he or she is wasting both time and money. Think again about the people who will use your product and where they are most likely to see an advertisement for your product.

Now, create your advertisement in this space. Remember, an ad does not always need very many words, and it can also use images. It just has to persuade.

Lesson 7 What Is the Writing Process?

Good writing starts with a plan. Good writers take certain steps, which make up the writing process. Following these five steps leads to better writing.

Step 1: Prewrite

Think of this as the time to discover and plan. Writers might choose a topic, or they might list everything they know about a topic already chosen. They might write down what they need to learn about a topic. Writers might make lists that contain sentences, words, or even pictures. Some writers might make a chart or table and begin to put their ideas in order.

Step 2: Draft

Writers put their ideas on paper. This first draft should contain sentences and paragraphs. Good writers keep their prewriting ideas nearby. There will be mistakes in this draft, and that's okay.

Step 3: Revise

Writers change or fix their first draft. They move ideas around, put them in a different order, or add information. They make sure they used clear words that really show what they mean. This is also the time to take out ideas that are not on topic.

Step 4: Proofread

Writers usually write a neat, new copy. Then, they look again to make sure everything is correct. They look especially for capital letters, end marks, and words that are not spelled correctly.

Step 5: Publish

Finally, writers make a final copy that has no mistakes. They are now ready to share their writing. There are many ways for writers to publish their work.

Lesson 7 What Is the Writing Process?

What does the writing process look like? Harlan used the writing process to write a paragraph about recess. His writing steps, below, are out of order. Label each step with a number and the name of the step.

Step _____ : _____
_____ The students at Weston Elementary need more recess. Lunch recess is only 20 mintes long. My dad read an artical about recess. Some people think that if we had another recess in the afternoon, we would pay better attention in class.

Step _____ : _____
_____ We need more recess. Lunch recess is only 20 mintes long. Some people think that if we had another recess in the afternoon, we would pay better attention in class. My dad read an artical about it.

Step _____ : _____
The students at Weston Elementary
_____ We need more recess. Lunch recess is only 20 mintes long. Some people think that if we had another recess in the afternoon, we would pay better attention in class. My dad read an artical about it.

Step _____ : _____
lunch recess should be longer
need afternoon recess
pay attention in class

Step _____ : _____
_____ The students at Weston Elementary need more recess. Lunch recess is only 20 minutes long. My dad read an article about recess. Some people think that if we had another recess in the afternoon, we would pay better attention in class.

Lesson 8 The Writing Process: Opinion Statement

Do you have an opinion about recess, school uniforms, or what gets served in the school cafeteria? An opinion statement is your opportunity to express your opinion. Follow the writing process to create an opinion statement.

Prewrite

First, think of some topics about which you have strong opinions. It might be a topic as big as world peace or as little as the new paint color in the school bathrooms. List some topics here.

_____   _____

_____   _____

Now, look over those topics and decide which one you want to write about. You should be able to explain your opinion and several supporting statements in a paragraph. Write the topic that you decide on here.

Topic for opinion statement: _____

Use this cluster map to record your opinion and all of its related ideas. Add more ovals to the diagram, as needed.

Lesson 8 The Writing Process: Opinion Statement

As a final step in the prewriting stage, organize your ideas into a main topic and several supporting statements. In this case, your main topic is the statement of your opinion.

Topic sentence: _____

Supporting idea: _____

Supporting idea: _____

Supporting idea: _____

Draft

Refer to your prewriting notes as you write a first draft. Remember, this is the time to get your ideas down on paper in sentences. You will have the chance to revise and proofread your writing later.

_____

_____

_____

_____

_____

_____

_____

_____

_____

Lesson 8 The Writing Process: Opinion Statement

Revise

Even the most famous writers create first drafts and then change them. Answer these questions about your draft. If you answer "no" to any of these questions, then those areas might need improvement.

- Did you state your opinion clearly in a topic sentence?

- Did you include details that support your topic sentence (your opinion)?

- Did you present your supporting statements in a logical order?

- Is each sentence a complete thought?

- Did you use clear words that really say what you mean?

Rewrite your opinion statement here. Make changes to improve your message, based on the questions you just answered.

_____

_____

_____

_____

_____

_____

_____

_____

Lesson 8 The Writing Process: Opinion Statement

Proofread

Your opinion statement is almost finished. Now, check it for any last little errors. It is best to check for one kind of error at a time. Proofread your revision on page 32. Use this checklist to help you catch all of the errors.

- Does each sentence begin with a capital letter?

- Does each sentence have an appropriate end mark?

- Are proper nouns capitalized?

- Are all words spelled correctly?

Publish

Write a final copy of your opinion statement here. Use your neatest printing or handwriting.

_____

_____

_____

_____

_____

_____

_____

_____

_____

Chapter 3

Lesson 1 What Is a Personal Narrative?

Have you ever written a true story about something that happened to you? If so, you were writing a personal narrative. A **personal narrative** is a true story an author writes about his or her own experiences.

Macy wrote a personal narrative about visiting her grandparents.

> **Over the River and Through the Woods**
>
> Last October, Mom, Dad, and I visited my grandparents in Wisconsin. They still live in the same house where Mom grew up. It took two days to drive from our house in North Carolina to theirs.
>
> All the way up, I was asking Mom to tell stories about winter there. She told me about giant snow banks and sliding parties. Once we got to Wisconsin, we ate lots of Grandma's good food and walked in the woods and looked at all the colorful trees. I tried to imagine the woods full of snow.
>
> Then, on Sunday evening, it started to snow. Big fluffy flakes floated down. They looked as if they were moving in slow motion. On Monday morning, when I looked out the window, I couldn't believe it. Grandpa said there were eight inches on the ground. Dad said we couldn't drive, and we would have to stay an extra day. Boy, was I glad!
>
> Grandma found one of my mother's old pairs of boots. I played outside in the snow all day. It was the best winter day I ever had!

Here are the features of a personal narrative:

- It tells a story about something that happens in a writer's life.
- It is written in the first person, using words such as *I, me,* and *my*.
- It uses time and time-order words to tell events in a sequence.
- It expresses the writer's personal feelings.

NAME _____

Lesson 1 What Is a Personal Narrative?

Why do people write personal narratives?

They might want to share their thoughts and feelings about something that happened to them. They might want to entertain their readers. Often, people write to share their experiences and to entertain.

Who reads personal narratives?

If you write a personal narrative, teachers, parents, and classmates might read it. As you think about your audience, ask yourself what you want to share with your readers. What might they learn about you?

What can personal narratives be about?

They can be about anything that actually happens to the author. It might be a happy or sad event, a goofy situation or a frightening one.

So, what could you write a personal narrative about? Here are some idea-starters. Look them over.

> my first dance lesson   how I met my best friend   my first day of school
> my greatest accomplishment   the thing of which I am most proud
> the thing that makes me angry   my earliest childhood memory
> my most embarrassing mistake

Write some notes about each idea-starter that interests you. One of these could be the start of a personal narrative.

Idea-starter: _____

_____

Idea-starter: _____

_____

Idea-starter: _____

_____

Lesson 2 Use Time Order

You already know that when you write instructions, the details need to be in order. Words such as *first*, *then*, *next*, and *last* help readers see and understand that order. In addition to those time-order words, **transition words** help readers know when things happen and in what order. Here are some common transition words.

after	as soon as	before	during	finally
later	meanwhile	second	soon	when

Circle the transition words when you find them.

After school, I thought that Jackie had gone home, so I went home, too. As soon as I got there, I knew something was wrong. The door was still locked. I was in a panic. After several terrible minutes, I remembered that Jackie was at her piano lesson.

Use some transition words in sentences.

Write about something that happened after something else.

_____

_____

Write about something that happens at the same time as something else.

_____

_____

Write about three things that happen in order.

_____

_____

Lesson 2 Use Time Order

In addition to time-order and transition words, writers can use **time words** to let readers know when things are happening. These words and phrases tell the time of day or the time of year, for example. Here are some time words and phrases. Add some more to the list.

noon	bedtime	in the morning
yesterday	November	two weeks ago

_____ _____ _____

_____ _____ _____

_____ _____ _____

Now, use some of the time words from the list. Write a sentence that might be part of a personal narrative. Use a time word or phrase at the beginning of your sentence.

_____

_____

Write a sentence about something that happened recently. Use a time word or phrase in the middle or at the end of your sentence.

_____

_____

Write a sentence about something that happens in a certain season. Name the season in your sentence.

_____

_____

Lesson 3 Use Vivid Verbs and Precise Nouns

Here is what you already know about verbs and nouns.

- A **verb** is an action word. *Jump, read,* and *turn* are examples of verbs.

- A **noun** names a person, place, thing, or idea. For example, *sister, barn, fireplace,* and *honesty* are nouns.

When writing, choose the best words to say what you want to say. Verbs and nouns are the key. If you choose them well, they will take you far.

A descriptive verb creates a picture in the reader's mind. It doesn't just tell what the action is, it really describes the action.

Here is an example.

He walked.

Look how changing the verb can change the sentence.

He shuffled.   He marched.

Both of those sentences really tell you something. If someone shuffles, maybe he is sick, or maybe he doesn't want to go wherever he is going. If someone marches, maybe he is a soldier or just very determined.

Write about how someone moves, but do not use the word *walk* or *run*. Try to create different moods or different feelings with the verbs you choose.

_____

_____

_____

_____

_____

Lesson 3 Use Vivid Verbs and Precise Nouns

A precise noun gives readers a better description than a general noun. For example, *car* is a general noun. But *sports car* would create a more precise, or specific, picture in readers' minds.

Here are some other general nouns. Can you think of more precise nouns to use instead of these?

people   shoe   tree   flower   building

Now, look at each sentence below. Each one contains a general noun. Rewrite the sentence and replace the general noun with a more precise noun. The first one is done for you.

The people ran around the track

<u>The joggers ran around the track.</u> _____

The flower in the bouquet smelled sweet.

_____

I had a terrible blister from my new shoe.

_____

I peeked through the dirty window of the building.

_____

The big, old tree had blown down in the wind.

_____

Write a sentence about people talking, but do not use any of these words: *people, talk, say,* or *said*. Use a descriptive verb and a precise noun.

_____

_____

Lesson 4 The Writing Process: Personal Narrative

A personal narrative does not have to be about an amazing rescue, a life-threatening accident, or a life-changing event. It can be about everyday things. Remember the narrative you read on page 34? Macy wrote about visiting her grandparents. A special thing happened while she was there, but it was neither amazing, life threatening, nor life-changing. It was just important to Macy.

Use the writing process to develop a personal narrative that is your own experience.

Prewrite

Look at the idea-starters on page 35 and the notes you made. Choose one of those ideas, or another idea that you like, and begin to work on it here.

My idea: _____

Use this idea web to collect and record details. Write down as many as you can.

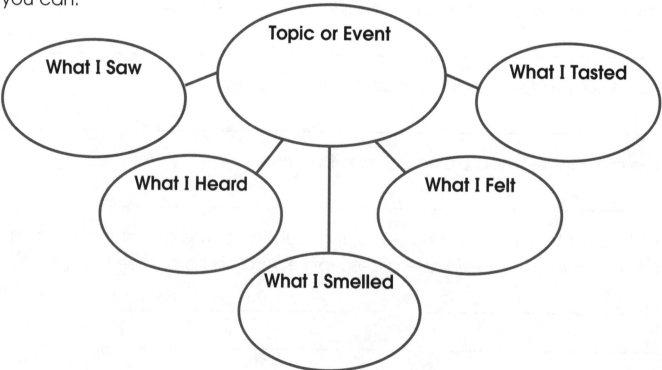

Lesson 4 The Writing Process: Personal Narrative

So far, you have chosen a topic and collected ideas. Now, it is time to put your ideas in order. Think about the story you are about to tell in your personal narrative. Use the sequence chart on this page to list the events in order. Do not worry about details here; just get the events down.

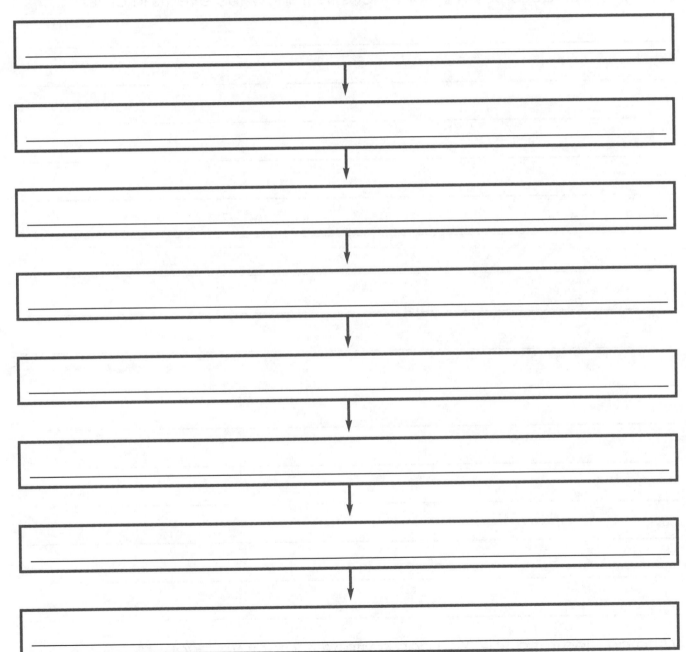

Lesson 4 The Writing Process: Personal Narrative

Draft

Use your sequence chart to help you write the first draft of your personal narrative on this page. As you write, do not worry about misspelled words. Just get your ideas down in sentences that show the events in order.

_____

_____

_____

_____

_____

_____

_____

_____

_____

_____

_____

_____

_____

_____

Write an idea for a title. You can change it later if you want to.

Title: _____

Lesson 4 The Writing Process: Personal Narrative

Revise

Almost every book you read has been revised many, many times before it even gets printed. It is hard, even for experienced writers, to change their work. However, it is necessary to look closely at a first draft and make sure that it is as good as it can be.

Answer the questions below about your draft. If you answer "no" to any of these questions, those areas might need improvement. Feel free to make marks on your draft so you know what needs more work.

- Did you tell about just one event in your narrative?

- Did you include details to make readers feel as if they are right there with you?

- Did you tell events in order? Did you use time and time-order words to show when events happened?

- Did you tell how you felt about the events? Do readers get a sense of your personal feelings?

- Did you use vivid verbs and precise nouns?

- Does your story flow well when you read it out loud?

Look back through your draft and underline the verbs. Do you use the same ones over and over? Do you use words that show the action? Here is an example of how Macy changed her work.

_____ Last October, Mom, Dad, and I ~~saw~~ visited my grandparents in Wisconsin.

They still live in the same house where Mom grew up. It took two days to

drive ~~go~~ from our house in North Carolina to theirs.

Lesson 4 The Writing Process: Personal Narrative

Write the revision of your first draft here. As you revise, remember to make sure your action words are really active and your nouns are precise!

_____

_____

_____

_____

_____

_____

_____

_____

_____

_____

_____

_____

_____

_____

_____

Are you still happy with your title? If not, write a new one here.

Title: _____

Lesson 4 The Writing Process: Personal Narrative

Proofread

Now is the time to correct those last little mistakes. Proofreading is easier if you look for one kind of error at a time. So, read through once for capital letters. Read again for end punctuation, and a third time for spelling. Here is a checklist to help you as you proofread your revised narrative.

_____ Each sentence begins with a capital letter.
_____ Each sentence ends with the correct punctuation (period, question mark, or exclamation point).
_____ Each sentence states a complete thought.
_____ All words are spelled correctly.

When proofreaders work, they use certain symbols. Using these symbols makes their job easier. They will make your job easier, too.

- Three little lines under a letter mean that the letter should be capitalized.

- If there is a period missing, do this⊙

- Can you insert a question mark like this?

- Do not forget your exclamation points!

- Fix misspelled words like tis.

Use these symbols as you proofread your personal narrative. Remember to read your writing out loud. Sometimes, you hear mistakes that you do not see.

Publish

Write a final copy of your personal narrative on a separate sheet of paper. Write carefully and neatly so that there are no mistakes.

Chapter 4
Lesson 1 Use Your Senses

If you were in this scene, you would learn about everything around you by using all five of your senses: sight, hearing, smell, touch, and taste. When you look at the picture, you have to imagine the sounds, smells, textures, and tastes.

When you write a description, you should also use all five of your senses, by using words that help readers use their senses.

Look again at the picture. What do you see? List some things here. Remember to help your reader see things, too. Do you see a tent, or a huge, striped tent?

What I see: _____   _____

_____   _____   _____

Now, use your other senses and write what you might hear, smell, touch, and taste in this scene.

What I hear: _____   _____

What I smell: _____   _____

What I touch: _____   _____

What I taste: _____   _____

Lesson 1 Use Your Senses

Look back at the lists you made on page 46. Did you remember to use descriptive sense words so that readers can see, hear, smell, touch, and taste what is in the scene, too? For example, if you said that you hear music, ask yourself what kind of music it might be. Is it loud music? Is it soothing music? Or is it "tinny-sounding" music? Review your lists and see if you can add any other words that more clearly describe the sights, sounds, smells, textures, and tastes.

Now, describe this scene so clearly that your reader will feel as if he or she is actually standing right in the middle of it. For this paragraph, organize your ideas by sense. First, write about what you saw. Then, write about what you heard, smelled, touched, and tasted. Remember to indent the first sentence of your paragraph.

_____

_____

_____

_____

_____

_____

_____

_____

_____

_____

_____

Lesson 2 Use Your Adjectives and Adverbs

You know that verbs and nouns are required to make a sentence. It takes just one of each to make a complete sentence. Adjectives and adverbs give sentences extra life.

> • An **adjective** is a word that describes a noun or pronoun. Adjectives tell *what kind, how much, how many*, and *which ones*. Adjectives tell how things look, sound, smell, feel, and taste.
>
> • An **adverb** is a word that describes either a verb, an adjective, or another adverb. Adverbs tell *how, when, where*, or *to what degree*. Many adverbs have the ending **-ly**, but some do not.

Notice how adjectives make a plain sentence more exciting.

The boy held books as he put on his coat.

What kind of boy was it? A little boy.

How many books did he hold? Three books.

What kind of coat was it? A red coat.

Here is the new sentence. Notice that the adjectives go right before the nouns that they describe. This is almost always true.

The little boy held three books as he put on his red coat.

Read the sentence below. Rewrite the sentence, adding two adjectives. Remember, an adjective tells more about a noun or pronoun.

The woman entered the room.

_____

NAME_____

Lesson 2 Use Your Adjectives and Adverbs

Start with the same sentence and see how adverbs make it more interesting. Remember, an adverb can describe a verb, an adjective, or another adverb.

   The boy held books as he put on his coat.

How did he hold the books? Carefully.

When did he put on his coat? Yesterday.

Here is the new sentence. Notice that the new adverbs are in different positions. One adverb is two words after the verb it describes. The other is four words after the verb it describes.

   The boy held books carefully as he put on his coat yesterday.

Look at each sentence below. Add information about *how, when, where,* or *to what degree* with an adverb. Write your new sentence on the line.

The woman entered the room.

_____

The horse stood at the fence and neighed.

_____

Now, improve these sentences by adding adjectives and adverbs that make the sentences more descriptive.

A cat slept in a patch of sunshine.

_____

Gerald cleared the table and put the dishes in the sink.

_____

Lesson 3 Organize It in Space

Writers use time order to tell about events. When writers describe objects or places, they use spatial order. They describe where things are. For example, they might describe an object from left to right or from top to bottom. Whichever order they go in, the idea is to give readers a clear picture of the object or place.

What is on the left in this picture? What is in the middle? What is on the right?

When organizing ideas by time, use time-order words. When organizing ideas by space, use words that tell where things are. Here are some common spatial words. Can you think of others?

above	across	beside	between	beyond	into	left
middle	next to	over	right		through	under

Look at a table, shelf, or another student's desk. Choose two objects that are in that place. Where are they? Are they next to each other? Is one on top of the other? Are they close or far away? Describe the two objects. In your description, write where they are.

_____

_____

On Your Own

Use spatial words to write riddles. Here is an example: What is hanging over the desk, next to the mirror? Challenge a friend or classmate to answer the riddle. Then, make up another one.

Lesson 3 Organize It in Space

When you enter a room, do your eyes usually go from side to side or from top to bottom? That might depend on what kind of room it is. If the room were in a normal home, you probably would look from side to side. If it were a cathedral in England, however, your eyes would probably be drawn to the high ceiling first, and then look downward. Remember to keep your audience in mind while writing.

Look at this mountain scene. Close your eyes and imagine that you are there. How can you help your classmates feel as if they are there, too? Describe the scene for them. Choose whether to organize your details from side to side or from top to bottom.

_____

_____

_____

_____

_____

_____

Lesson 4 How Do We Compare?

To compare two items, a Venn diagram is a useful tool. Tasha can not decide whether she prefers So-Soft peach shampoo or Kleen lime shampoo. She made a Venn diagram to compare the two products. She wrote things that are the same about the two products in the center. Things that are different about So-Soft are in the left circle, and things that are different about Kleen are in the right circle.

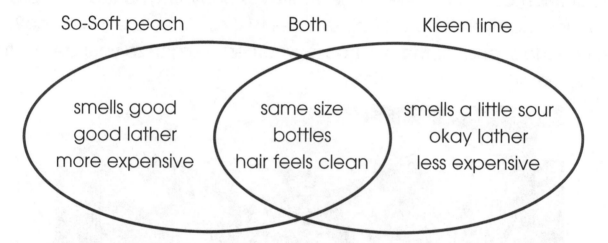

So-Soft peach   Both   Kleen lime

smells good   same size   smells a little sour
good lather   bottles   okay lather
more expensive   hair feels clean   less expensive

Start with a very basic comparison. Compare an apple and a playground ball. Write what is different about an apple in the left circle. Write what is different about a playground ball in the right circle. Write what is the same about both objects in the center.

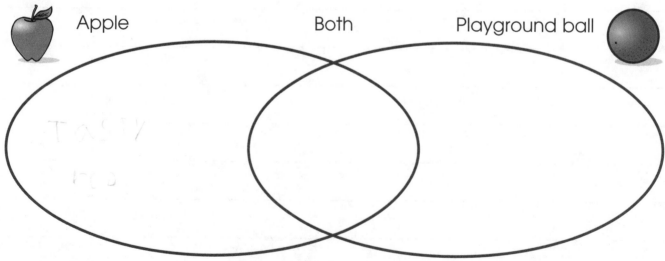

Apple   Both   Playground ball

Spectrum Writing
Grade 4
52

Chapter 4 Lesson 4
Descriptive Writing

Lesson 4 How Do We Compare?

What else would you like to compare? Maybe you want to compare two books you have read, two foods, or two products. Choose the items you want to compare and label the circles. Then, write what is the same and different about the items.

_____ Both _____

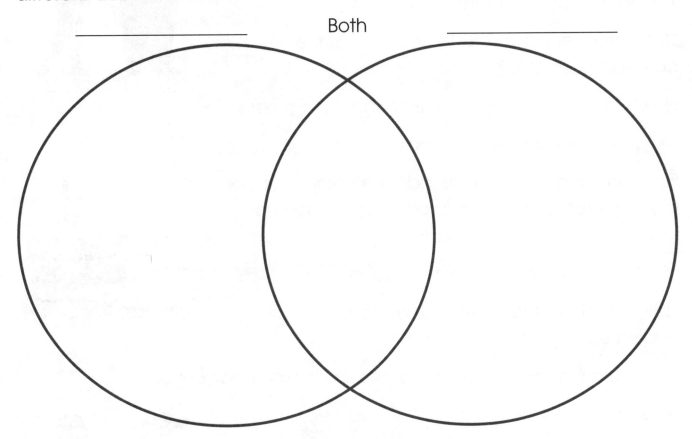

Now, use the information in your diagram to write some sentences.

Write a sentence that tells how your two items are the same.

_____

_____

In a sentence, name one way your two items are different.

_____

_____

Lesson 5 Compare Two and More Than Two

Comparing things tell how they are alike and different. The ending **-er** and the word *more* are used to talk and write about how two things are different.

Jack is *taller* than Jill.

Notice that **er** was added to the end of the comparing word *tall*.

Now, compare the children using the word *serious*.

Jill is **more** *serious* than Jack.

For short words, such as *tall*, add the ending **-er**. For longer words with three or more syllables, such as *serious*, use *more* to compare.

My sandwich is *thinner* than yours.

Notice that another **n** was added to *thin* before adding **er**.

You might also say my sandwich is *skimpier* than yours.

For *skimpy*, change the **y** to **i**, then add **er**.

Look at the pictures. Then, use the comparing words *sloppy*, *neat*, and *comfortable* to complete the sentences below.

Joe is _____ Dexter.

Dexter is _____ Joe.

Do you think Joe's clothes are _____ than Dexter's?

Lesson 5 Compare Two and More Than Two

To talk or write about how three or more things are different, use the ending **-est** or the word *most*.

Lou is the *smallest* rat.

Notice the spelling of *big* and *tiny* when the ending **-est** is added.

Linda is the *biggest* rat.   Lou is the *tiniest* rat.

Also, use *most* instead of adding *-est* to words three syllables or longer.

I think Lee is the **most** *beautiful* of the three.

Look at the pictures. Then, use the comparing words *big, small, gigantic,* and *wrinkly* in four sentences about the elephants.

_____

_____

_____

_____

Lesson 6 Compare Two Objects

When comparing, organize your ideas so the comparison is clear for the reader.

There are two ways to organize your writing when you compare things. One way is to talk first about one object, then about the other. Here is an example. Information about the first object is in red. Information about the second object is in blue.

> There are two bananas left in the fruit bowl. Which one should I eat? The first one is yellow. It feels very firm. The second one is black and badly bruised. It feels a little squishy.

The other way is to talk first about one feature, or characteristic, as it relates to both objects. Then, go on to another feature, and so on. Here is an example.

> There are two bananas left in the fruit bowl. Which one should I eat? The first one is yellow. The second is black and badly bruised. The first one feels very firm. The second one feels a little squishy when I touch it.

Compare a horse with a zebra. First, use this Venn diagram to collect details.

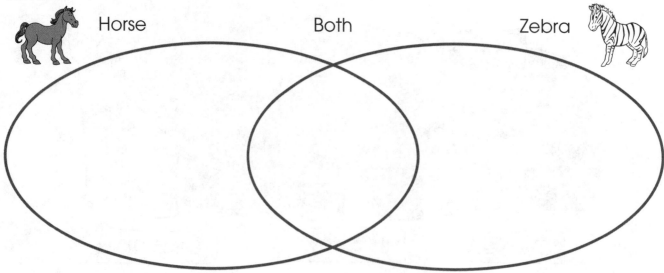

Horse   Both   Zebra

Lesson 6 Compare Two Objects

Write a paragraph comparing a horse with a zebra. Follow the first example paragraph on page 56 by first describing the horse, then the zebra.

_____

_____

_____

_____

_____

_____

_____

Now, write a paragraph comparing the same animals again. This time, though, organize your comparison feature by feature. For example, talk about the size of the animals, then talk about the colors of the animals, and so on.

_____

_____

_____

_____

_____

_____

Lesson 7 The Writing Process: Descriptive Writing

Descriptive writing plays a big part in both creative writing, such as stories, and formal writing, such as reports and personal accounts. Whenever writers want to make their readers "see" something, they use descriptive writing. Use the writing process to develop a paragraph that describes a place. It can be a real or made-up place.

Prewrite

First, think of some places and list them below. They might be pleasant places, like a sunny meadow, or not-so-pleasant places, such as a dark, smelly basement.

Real Places   Made-up Places

_____   _____

_____   _____

_____   _____

Now, look over your lists and think about the places. Which one do you think you can describe most vividly? Choose one and write the name below.

Place I will describe: _____

Use this idea web to collect and record details about your place.

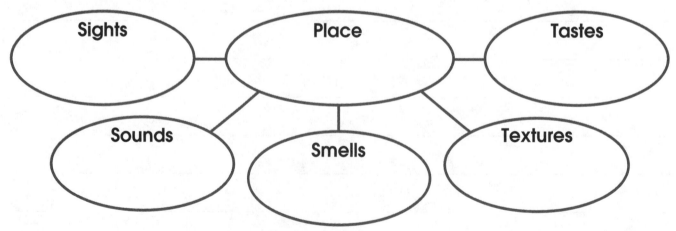

Lesson 7 The Writing Process: Descriptive Writing

As a final step in the prewriting stage, organize your ideas. Will you describe the place from left to right, top to bottom, near to far, or some other way? Remember to keep your audience in mind.

Method of organization: _____

Major details, in order:

Draft

Refer to your prewriting notes as you write a first draft. Remember, this is the time to get your ideas down on paper in sentences. You will check for mistakes later.

_____

_____

_____

_____

_____

_____

Lesson 7 The Writing Process: Descriptive Writing

Revise

Answer these questions about your draft. If you answer "no" to any of these questions, then those areas might need improvement.

- Did you keep your audience in mind? Did you include details that will interest them and that they will understand?

- Did you make your first sentence especially interesting so that readers will want to continue?

- Did you use spatial words to show where things are?

- Did you use vivid verbs and precise nouns to help readers see the place?

- Did you use sense words? To how many of your readers' senses did you appeal?

Revise your description here. Make changes to improve your message based on the questions you just answered.

_____

_____

_____

_____

_____

_____

_____

Lesson 7 The Writing Process: Descriptive Writing

Proofread

Your description should be in good shape now. The last task is to check it for any last little errors. It is best to check for one kind of error at a time. Proofread your revision on page 60. Use this checklist to help you catch all of the errors.

_____ Does each sentence begin with a capital letter?
_____ Does each sentence have an appropriate end mark?
_____ Are proper nouns capitalized?
_____ Are all words are spelled correctly?

Publish

Write a final copy of your description. Use your best printing or handwriting.

_____

_____

_____

_____

_____

_____

_____

_____

_____

_____

Chapter 5

Lesson 1 What Makes a Story?

You probably know many, many stories. If someone asked, would you be able to tell what a story is?

- A story tells about made-up people or animals. They are the **characters** in the story.
- A story has a **setting** where the action takes place.
- A story has a **plot**, or series of events, with a problem that needs to be solved.
- A story uses **dialogue**, or conversation among the characters, to move the action of the story along.
- An interesting **beginning**, **middle**, and **end** make a story fun to read.
- **Describing words** tell about the characters, setting, and events.

Leaf Dash

"Come on out, Charlotte," Charlie called to his sister. He wanted to play Leaf Dash. The trick was not to let the leaves crackle under your feet.

"Are you sure there aren't any dogs out here?" she asked, nervously peering out from the burrow.

"I couldn't be more sure," answered Charlie. "You're it!" he called as he ran off. Charlotte, unable to resist a good game, went off in pursuit.

They played until the sun was high in the sky. The game was especially good because the leaves were really piling up in the dry creek bed. Charlotte didn't even think about dogs until she heard a loud crackling sound beyond the next rock. Charlie was really good at not making the leaves crackle. Maybe he was trying to fool her.

"Charlie, is that you?" Charlotte's voice squeaked a little. There was no answer. She tried again. "Charlie, I hear you. Come on out."

Just then, a dog's large brown head and pointy ears appeared over the rock. Charlotte froze for a moment, then turned and ran for the burrow. Leaves crunched under her own feet as she dashed, but she didn't care. All that she wanted was her safe burrow.

Lesson 1 What Makes a Story?

> She leaped the last few inches into the burrow and tripped over Charlie. Charlie was laughing.
>
> "What do you think is so funny?" demanded Charlotte, in between gulps of air.
>
> Charlie stopped laughing and bowed to Charlotte. "The Leaf Dash prize is all yours, my dear sister. I never saw anyone move so fast!"

Answer these questions about "Leaf Dash." Look back at the story if you need to.

Who are the characters in the story?

_____   _____

Where does the action take place? What words in the story told you?

Setting: _____

Words from the story: _____ _____ _____

What problem occurs?

_____

_____

Charlie answers Charlotte's question with, "I couldn't be more sure." Do you think Charlie is a shy chipmunk or a bold chipmunk? Why?

_____

_____

_____

The writer uses words that appeal to readers' senses. Write some of those sense words here.

_____ _____ _____

Lesson 2 Practice Your Dialogue

Dialogue is the conversation between characters in a story. Dialogue makes a story's characters seem more real. Here is what dialogue looks like.

> "Does everyone agree with my idea of holding a car wash to raise money for charity?" Carl asked. The whole class just sat there. "Does anyone have a better idea?" he asked impatiently.
>
> One hand went up. It was Dalton. Carl nodded at him and said, "Yeah?"
>
> "I…um, I had an idea," Dalton began. He cleared his throat and tried again. "Well, it's probably a dumb idea, but I thought maybe, if anyone else thought it was a good idea, that we could raise money by having a read-a-thon."

Take a closer look at a line of dialogue.

Quotation marks go before and after the speaker's exact words.

"I…um, I had an idea," Dalton began.

A **comma** separates the speaker's words from the tag line.

The **tag line** tells who is speaking.

Add the punctuation to the dialogue below. Look at the story above for examples if you need help.

1. That sounds like a good idea responded Taylor.

2. Eve asked What is a read-a-thon?

3. Dalton, why don't you tell everyone said Taylor.

Dialogue can tell more than what characters say. Readers learn about characters both by what they say and by how they say it. You also learn about a character from what other characters say about him or her. Dialogue keeps readers interested and moves the story along.

Lesson 2 Practice Your Dialogue

Dialogue should sound like real people talking. A nine-year-old character should sound like a kid. A mayor should sound like a mayor. It would not seem right to have a kid say something like, "Hello, Justin. It's so good to see you. How is your family?" A kid sounds more like, "Hey, Justin. How ya doin'?"

Write a conversation between the two characters described below. Make sure it sounds right, based on the information about each character. Remember to use quotation marks and tag lines. Look at the examples on page 64 if you need to.

Character 1: Mr. Alonzo Silva, age 56, the head of the town government

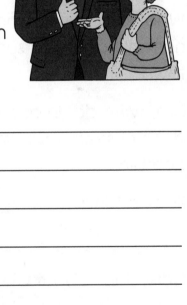

Character 2: Martin Shiller, age 10, newspaper delivery boy, wants to complain to the town government because the sidewalks are in poor condition, which makes it hard for him to deliver his newspapers

_____

_____

_____

_____

_____

_____

_____

_____

Lesson 3 Imagine a Setting

Dialogue helps readers learn about the characters. It also helps the story move along. What does the setting of a story do?

A story's setting helps set the tone, or mood, of a story. That is why scary scenes in movies and television shows often take place during rainstorms or at night. Those settings—rainstorms and nighttime—add interest and excitement to the action.

What kind of a setting can you imagine for a great story? Is it a perfectly normal home in a suburb or an abandoned warehouse on the edge of town?

First, write down as many ideas for story settings as you can. Even if an idea doesn't seem really interesting, write it anyway. You might end up combining ideas.

Setting ideas: _____ _____

_____ _____ _____

Now, think about when your great story will take place: in the past, in the present, or in the future. Read over your setting ideas again. Imagine each place in the past, present, and future. Which idea seems most interesting? Write your favorite idea here.

Place: _____   Time: _____

Lesson 3 Imagine a Setting

Now, it is time to fill out your setting. What is there to see? What sounds and smells are there? What textures and tastes?

Sights: _____

_____

Sounds: _____

_____

Smells: _____

_____

Textures: _____

_____

Tastes: _____

_____

Review the details you have written. Can you really imagine the place?

Now, describe the setting of your story. Remember to organize your details in a way that makes sense. For example, if you are describing a room, you might go from left to right. If you are describing the inside of a huge cave, you might go from bottom to top. If you are describing an outdoor setting, you might go from near to far. Use the method that makes the most sense for your setting.

_____

_____

_____

_____

Lesson 4 Create a Character

You have read many books and some of them probably had great characters in them. Do you remember cheering for them or feeling bad when things went wrong? Write down the names of some characters you remember from stories and books you have read.

_____   _____

_____   _____

When reading, you learn about characters in a number of different ways.

- What the narrator says.
- What the character says and how he or she says it.
- What the character does.
- What other characters say about the character.

Look at your list of characters again. Choose one that you remember especially well. Write what you know about that character. What kind of person is he or she? What do other characters think about him or her?

Character: _____

What I know about this character: _____

_____

_____

Now, think of a character you would like to write about. Rather than thinking about what happens to the character, think about what kind of person the character is. Answer these questions.

Is the character human? _____ If not, what is the character? _____

Is the character male or female? _____

Lesson 4 Create a Character

Circle the word in each pair that best describes your character:

bold / (shy) (hopeful) / defeated (decisive) / wishy-washy

(active) / passive (clever) / not very clever (strong) / weak

What background details or family history might be important to readers?

_____

_____

What might your character say? How might your characters say it? Write a line of dialogue that your character might speak.

_____

_____

What might other characters say about this character? Either show some dialogue or describe what others would say.

_____

_____

Now, introduce your character. Write a paragraph about him or her.

_____

_____

_____

_____

_____

_____

NAME _____

Lesson 5 What's Your Point of View?

The **point of view** in a story is who tells the story. The writer writes the story, but who is the narrator who tells the story?

In some stories, the narrator is one of the characters. These stories use words such as *I, me*, and *my* to let the reader know that this is happening. This is called **first-person point of view**. Here is a small piece of a story written in first person.

> "Why were you so late coming home from school, Lou?" Mom asked.
> I scuffed my toe against the shiny kitchen floor. I looked at the ceiling. I looked out the window. I looked everywhere but at Mom. How could I tell her that I had gotten into trouble? Maybe she wouldn't ask too many questions if I told her part of the truth.
> "Well, I stayed after to talk to Mr. Hutchins for a while," I said, but I knew she would only ask why.

Here is the same story, but it is written in **third-person point of view**. The narrator is not a character in the story. Instead, the narrator sees and hears all the action, but does not take part in it. Third-person stories use words such as *he, she, him, her, his, they*, and *them*.

> "Why were you so late coming home from school, Lou?" Mom asked.
> Lou scuffed his toe against the shiny kitchen floor. He looked at the ceiling. He looked out the window. He looked everywhere but at his mom. How could he tell her that he had gotten into trouble? Maybe she wouldn't ask too many questions if he told her part of the truth.
> "Well, I stayed after to talk to Mr. Hutchins for a while," he said, but he knew she would only ask why.

Lesson 5 What's Your Point of View?

Look back at the piece of the story on page 70. What do you think Lou's mom was thinking during this conversation? Rewrite this part of the story from the first-person point of view, with Mom as the narrator. The first sentence is done for you.

"Why were you so late coming home from school, Lou?" I asked.

_____

_____

_____

_____

_____

_____

Now, practice writing in third-person point of view. What happens next? Does Mom ask more questions? Does Lou lie, or does he tell the truth? Write the next part of the conversation in third-person point of view.

_____

_____

_____

_____

_____

_____

_____

Lesson 6 Stories Are Everywhere

Do you like stories about aliens or about animals that talk? Stories like these are called **fantasy**. Their characters could not be real, and the events could not actually happen.

List some stories or books you have read that are fantasies.

_____   _____

_____   _____

What kind of fantasy would you like to write? Will you set it in the city or in the country? Does the story happen on Earth or some other planet? Perhaps your character is a talking tree or has a special power of some sort. Let your imagination go and write down a couple of fantasy story ideas here.

Fantasy idea #1

Character(s): _____

Setting: _____

Plot: _____

Fantasy idea #2

Character(s): _____

Setting: _____

Plot: _____

Fantasy idea #3

Character(s): _____

Setting: _____

Plot: _____

Lesson 6 Stories Are Everywhere

Many stories that you read include human characters. They are normal people who live on Earth, whether in the past or present. These stories are called **realistic**. Though the characters come from a writer's imagination, they could be real, and the story's events could actually happen.

List some stories or books you have read that are realistic.

_____   _____

_____   _____

What kind of realistic story would you like to write? It could be about something sad or funny that happens to an ordinary kid. It might be about a family whose vacation goes completely wrong. Realistic stories require just as much imagination as fantasies do. Write down some realistic story ideas.

Realistic story idea #1

Character(s): _____

Setting: _____

Plot: _____

Realistic idea #2

Character(s): _____

Setting: _____

Plot: _____

Lesson 7 The Writing Process: Story

In a story, you can recreate your own world or create an entirely new world. You can write about things that have happened to you, or you can write about events you can only imagine. Use the writing process to see just what kind of a world you can create.

Prewrite

Read the story ideas you developed on pages 72 and 73. Choose one of those ideas, or another idea that you like, and begin to develop it. Pay special attention to your character here. Use this idea web to record details about how he or she looks, acts, speaks, and other details.

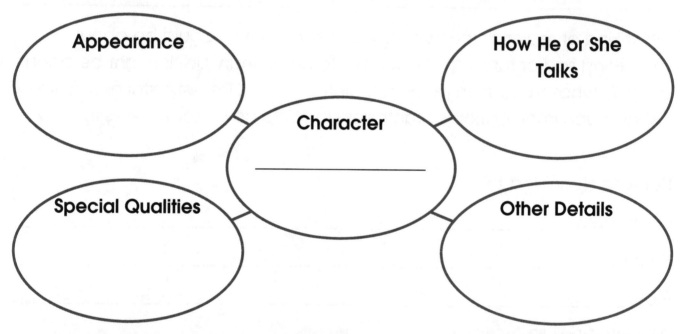

Before you go on, consider these questions about your setting and plot.

- What is the setting of your story? (Think about place or location, season, time of day, weather conditions, and so on.)

- What is the character's problem?

- What does the character do to try to solve the problem? Does it take more than one try?

Lesson 7 The Writing Process: Story

Now, it is time to put the parts of your story together. Think about the story you are about to tell. Use the story map on this page to list the important parts of your story.

Character(s)

_____

Setting

_____

Plot: Beginning

_____

_____

_____

Plot: Middle

_____

_____

_____

Plot: End

_____

_____

_____

Lesson 7 The Writing Process: Story

Draft

It is time to write a first draft of your story. Write your draft below, using your story map to help you. Don't worry about misspelling words or getting everything perfect. Just get your ideas down in sentences and in order.

_____

_____

_____

_____

_____

_____

_____

_____

_____

_____

_____

_____

_____

_____

Write an idea for a title here. It might change later, but that's okay.

Title: _____

Lesson 7 The Writing Process: Story

Revise

When you write a story, you work hard to make it good. It is very hard to go back and ask yourself, "How can I make it better?" Answer the questions below about your draft. If you answer "no" to any of these questions, those are the areas that might need improvement. Feel free to make marks on your draft on page 76.

- Did you give details about an interesting character and a setting?
- Did you include a problem and a solution in your plot?
- Did you tell events in an order that makes sense?
- Did you create pictures in your readers' minds with well-chosen words?
- Did you use dialogue to help readers learn about characters and to move the story forward?
- Did you describe how things look, sound, smell, feel, and taste?
- Did you use sentences of different lengths and styles?

Now, review the important parts of a story.

- In the beginning of a story, readers meet the characters and learn a little about the setting and the plot. The first sentence of a story should make readers want to keep on reading.

- In the middle of a story, the action takes place. Characters face their problem. They make one or more attempts to solve the problem.

- In the end, the characters solve the problem in a logical way. It is not very satisfying to read a story in which a big problem just "goes away." Make sure that your characters really work to solve the problem.

On your draft, draw brackets around the beginning, middle, and end of your story. Write some notes if you decide to change any of those parts to make them more interesting for your readers.

Lesson 7 The Writing Process: Story

Write the revision of your first draft here. As you revise, remember to make your characters say things that sound natural.

_____

_____

_____

_____

_____

_____

_____

_____

_____

_____

_____

_____

_____

Are you still happy with your title? If not, now is your chance to change it.

Title: _____

Lesson 7 The Writing Process: Story

Proofread

Now is the time to correct those last little mistakes. Proofreading is easier if you look for just one kind of error at a time. So, read through once for capital letters. Read for end punctuation and then for spelling.

_____ Each sentence begins with a capital letter.
_____ Each sentence ends with the correct punctuation (period, question mark, or exclamation point).
_____ Dialogue is punctuated correctly.
_____ Each sentence states a complete thought.
_____ All words are spelled correctly.

When proofreaders work, they use certain symbols. Using these symbols makes their job easier. They will make your job easier, too.

- three little lines under a letter mean that something should be capitalized.

- Write in a missing end mark like this: ⊙ ? !

- "Please add a comma and quotation marks" she said.

- Fix incorrect or misspelled words like these.

Use these symbols as you proofread your story. Remember to read your writing out loud. Sometimes, you hear mistakes or rough spots that you do not see.

Publish

Write a final copy of your story on a separate sheet of paper. Write carefully and neatly so that there are no mistakes. Then, draw illustrations and make a nice cover or title page. Share your story with friends and family.

Chapter 6
Lesson 1 When and Why Do We Persuade?

Have you ever seen an advertisement? Well, of course you have. Thousands of them! Advertisements are persuading you. They are trying to make you think in a certain way or take a certain action.

"The Best Doggone Dog Food Around."

Have you ever tried to talk a friend into going somewhere with you? Maybe you tried to talk a parent into playing a game. If you did those things, you were persuading. You were trying to get someone to think in a certain way or to take a certain action.

In persuasive writing, writers try to make readers think, feel, or act in a certain way. Remember, advertisements are one form of persuasive writing. Letters to the editor are another. People usually write letters to the editor to state an opinion. Their hope is that other people will come to think in the same way and, perhaps, take action.

> Dear Editor:
>   There are children and adults in our community who go hungry. The local food pantry meets the needs of only some of those people. On Saturday, November 4th, volunteers will hold a yard sale to benefit the food pantry. To donate items, deliver them before Saturday to the back door of the pantry at 621 Carver St. With good community support, the food pantry will raise enough money to supply food to many other families through the winter months. I hope you will support this worthy cause.
>
> J. Adkins
> Worthington

Lesson 1 When and Why Do We Persuade?

In the letter to the editor on page 80, the writer states some facts. She informs her readers about an event that will soon occur. She tells why the event is being held. At the end, she tells people exactly what she wants them to do: "support this worthy cause." Notice that at the same time, she states her opinion. It is her opinion that it is a worthy cause.

Imagine that you have a job, and you feel that you should be paid more than you are getting. Your opinion, in this case, is "I deserve a raise." Your job, in the persuasive part, is to give your boss reasons why you deserve the raise. At the end, you should tell your boss just what action you hope he or she will take. Remember to keep your audience in mind. This is perhaps especially important with persuasive writing. An employee would be respectful toward a boss. Think hard about how to make your boss want to give you a raise.

Dear Boss:

Lesson 2 Give Me the Facts

Can you persuade someone to believe as you do simply because you state an opinion? Probably not. You must give reasons, or facts, to support your opinions. It is the facts that do the persuading for us.

A **fact** is something known to be true or real or something that can be proven true.

An **opinion** is a belief or a personal judgment.

Look at another letter to the editor from a concerned citizen. Think about which statements are facts and which are opinions.

Dear Editor:

I think it's shameful that some people in our nice community don't have enough to eat. The food pantry on Carver Street shouldn't have to solve that problem all by itself. It is run entirely by volunteers.

The city should help to solve this problem. The pantry had a yard sale on Saturday. We shouldn't have to be holding yard sales to make sure that people have enough food.

B. Tranton
Worthington

Write two statements from the letter that are facts.

_____

_____

_____

Write two statements from the letter that are opinions.

_____

_____

_____

Lesson 2 Give Me the Facts

Opinions often use words such as these:

I think   I believe   most   should

must   ought   never   always   in my opinion

When reading, watch for words that identify opinions. Look back at the letter to the editor on page 82. Circle the opinion words that you find there.

Now, write a letter in response to B. Tranton's letter about the community's food pantry and the problem of providing food for people who don't have enough. You may make up facts to support your opinion. Make sure that they are facts, though, and not just more opinions.

Dear Editor:

I am writing in response to B. Tranton's letter, which was printed in the newspaper on Tuesday, November 8.

_____

_____

_____

_____

_____

_____

_____

_____

_____

_____

Lesson 3 Don't Make Me Cry

When writing persuasively, some writers appeal to readers' emotions to get them to think, feel, or act in a certain way. This method, called an *emotional appeal*, is used by advertisers as well as by people who write opinion statements or letters to the editor.

Look at these advertising slogans. They are all examples of emotional appeals.

Harding Furniture—We have your comfort in mind

Oatmeal To Go–Just like Grandma used to make

O'Malley's–Where eating out is like coming home

In all three cases, the advertisers try to make their readers feel good. They appeal to readers' feelings about comfort, family, and home.

Write your own emotional appeal. Create a slogan for a restaurant.

_____

The key to an emotional appeal is to hit on something that people feel strongly about. For example, people feel strongly about good health, their family's well-being, and their favorite sports teams. They also feel strongly about high prices, natural disasters, and people who do bad things. So, emotional appeals may tie into positive feelings or negative feelings.

In this letter to the editor, a writer appeals to negative emotions in the first sentence to persuade readers to believe as he does.

> The people who made this decision must be criminals. Removing the stoplight by the elementary school is just an accident waiting to happen. There is nothing to protect the children who cross that street before and after school.

Lesson 3 Don't Make Me Cry

Choose a product or type of business from those listed in the box. Then, come up with two possible slogans or statements about the business. In each box, write an emotional appeal.

| video store | bike helmets | dentist office |
| children's shoes | mattress store | fabric shop |

Now, write an emotional appeal in a letter to the editor. Choose one of the following topics. Make an emotional appeal and ask your readers to take some action.

| community clean-up | neighborhood crime | 4th of July celebration |
| traffic tie-ups | new city park | the mayor's poor choice of ties |

_____
_____
_____
_____

Lesson 4 Find Your Active Voice

Usually, the subject of a sentence does the action. That is easy to see in this sentence:

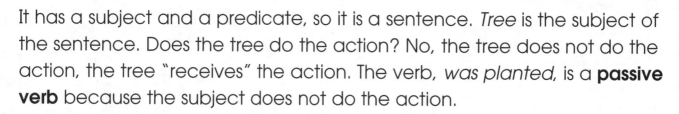

Ellie *planted* a tree.

The verb in the sentence is an **active verb** because the subject does the action.

What about this sentence?

A tree *was planted*.

It has a subject and a predicate, so it is a sentence. *Tree* is the subject of the sentence. Does the tree do the action? No, the tree does not do the action, the tree "receives" the action. The verb, *was planted*, is a **passive verb** because the subject does not do the action.

Passive verbs are always two-part verbs. They always have a helping verb, *am*, *is*, *was*, *be*, or *been*, plus a main verb. That does not mean that whenever you see one of those helping verbs that the verb is passive.

Passive verb: Cher *was called* to the office.
Active verb: Cher *was calling* for help.

How can you tell the difference? Ask yourself these two questions:

What is the subject?
Is the subject doing the action?

If the answer to the second question is "yes," then you have an active verb. If the answer is "no," you have a passive verb.

Why does it matter? Sometimes, you have to use passive verbs when you write. Maybe you do not know who did the action, so you have to say, "The goal was scored." Most of the time, however, your writing will be more clear and easier to read if you use active verbs.

Lesson 4 Find Your Active Voice

Compare these two paragraphs. One uses mostly active verbs and the other uses mostly passive verbs. Identify which is which.

A big job has been tackled by the fourth-graders at Braxton School. The old nature trail in the woods behind the school has been cleared out. Weeds were pulled by some students. Young trees were cut by others. The students are to be thanked for their hard work.	The fourth-graders at Braxton School tackled a big job. They cleared out the old nature trail in the woods behind the school. Some students pulled weeds. Others cut young trees. We thank the students for their hard work.
_____	_____

Underline the subject of each sentence below. Put an **X** next to each sentence that contains a passive verb.

_____ Jae was glad to pull weeds.

_____ Dandelions have very long roots.

_____ The pile of weeds was carted away.

_____ The trail was opened the next day.

Practice writing sentences with active verbs. First, look at the sentences above that have passive verbs. Rewrite one of those sentences with an active verb. If you need to, add a subject, such as *I* or *we* to the sentence.

_____

Now, write a new sentence about a tree. Make sure you use an active verb.

_____

Lesson 5 Organize by Importance

When writing about an event, use time order. When describing a place, use spatial order. When writing to persuade, you should use **order of importance**.

Remember, when writing to persuade, you try to make your readers think or act in a certain way. For example, you might try to persuade classmates to vote for having a pizza party instead of an ice cream party on the last day of school. You might try to persuade a teacher that the class needs more playground equipment.

When you write to persuade, you should save your most important ideas, your strongest arguments, for last. So, build your ideas from least important to most important. Now, read about this playground equipment problem.

> We, the students in Mr. DeCarlo's class, feel that we need new playground equipment. Our equipment is left over from last year, and most of the few pieces we have are damaged. One basketball has a gash and the other is flat. The two soccer balls are also damaged. That leaves just one football and one jump rope. We understand that each classroom is responsible for its own set of equipment. We promise to take good care of any new equipment our class gets. Having better playground equipment will help us to get more exercise at recess.

This writer gave several reasons for why the class should have new equipment. Number them in the paragraph. Then, underline the most important reason.

Lesson 5 Organize by Importance

What does your classroom need? More art supplies? New bookshelves? More playground equipment? Write a letter to your teacher or principal. Try to persuade the person that you really do need the item or items. Save your strongest, or most important, reason for last.

Before you begin drafting your letter, write your reasons here. Then, number them in the order you will use them in your paragraph.

Reason: _____

Reason: _____

Reason: _____

Reason: _____

Dear _____,

_____

_____

_____

_____

_____

_____

_____

_____

_____

Lesson 6 Just Business

A business letter is one you write to a company, organization, or a person you do not know. Business letters are usually written

- to make a request.

- to express a concern.

- to make a complaint.

Business letters often want the recipient to do something, so there is usually an element of persuasion. Read this business letter. Notice its six parts.

> The **heading** includes the sender's address and the date.

744 Douglas Avenue
Hartford, CT 06114
November 14, 2008

> The **inside address** is the recipient's name and address.

Customer Service Department
American Playground Company
1601 N. 44th Street
Milwaukee, WI 53208

> The **greeting** is followed by a colon.

Dear Customer Service Department:

> The text of the letter is the **body**.

   Melton Elementary School recently ordered playground equipment from your company. Our purchase order was No. 174346. Upon receiving the shipment, we discovered two problems. First, we had ordered 15 seven-foot jump ropes, but received only 14. Second, two of the soccer balls have cracks in them and are not holding air.

   Please ship an additional seven-foot jump rope and two replacement soccer balls so that our order is complete. Thank you for your prompt attention to this matter.

> The **closing** is followed by a comma.

Cordially,

Marta Alvarez

> The sender always includes a **signature**.

Marta Alvarez, Principal

Lesson 6 Just Business

Label the six parts of this business letter. Add the appropriate punctuation to the greeting and the closing.

_____

_____

_____

_____

_____

744 Douglas Avenue
Hartford, CT 06114
November 15, 2008

Mr. Andrew Martinsen
Principal, Melton Elementary School
854 Elizabeth Avenue
Salem, OR 97303

Dear Mr. Martinsen

    I discovered your school by accident on the Internet the other day. It seems we are both the principal of a Melton Elementary School. What a coincidence!

    My Melton students would love to know what your Melton students are doing. The teachers have many ideas, such as sharing and comparing daily weather forecasts, matching up pen pals, and so on. And we would love to hear your ideas as well.

    Please call me at your convenience. I am eager to talk about the possibilities. This seems like a great chance to connect your Oregon students with my Connecticut students.

Cordially

Marta Alvarez

Marta Alvarez
Principal, Melton Elementary School

Lesson 7 The Writing Process: Letter to the Editor

Use the writing process to create a letter to the editor. State an opinion about your school or community.

Prewrite

Think of some issues about which you have strong feelings. They might be related to conditions or rules at your school. They might be related to things going on in your community. They might have to do with larger issues, such as global warming or people's rights. Write down a few issues.

_____   _____

_____   _____

Now, think about those issues for a few minutes. Is there one that you think might interest others in your community? Choose one about which you are comfortable expressing your opinion. Write your choice here.

_____

Use this idea web to collect your thoughts and feelings about this issue. Remember, your goal is to get your audience to think or act in a certain way. With what do you want them to agree? What action do you want them to take? What reasons must you provide to accomplish this?

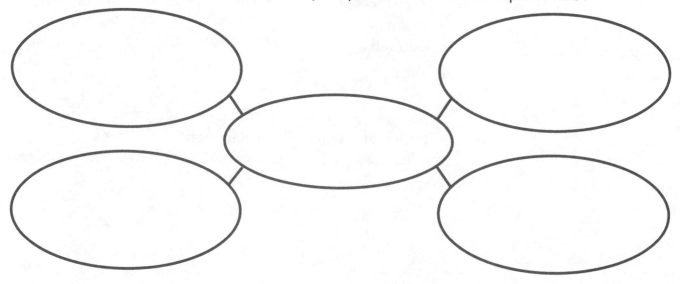

NAME _____

Lesson 7 The Writing Process: Letter to the Editor

Now, it is time to organize the points you will make in your letter. Save your strongest argument for last. Write your important reasons or points in order in these boxes.

1. _____
   _____
   _____

2. _____
   _____
   _____

3. _____
   _____
   _____

4. _____
   _____
   _____

5. _____
   _____
   _____

Lesson 7 The Writing Process: Letter to the Editor

Draft

It is time to write a first draft of your letter. Format it as a letter to the editor of your local newspaper. Look back at page 90 to review the business letter format. Keep the chart on page 93 nearby. As you write, don't worry about misspelling words or getting everything perfect. Just write your ideas down in sentences and in order from least to most important.

_____

_____

_____

_____

_____

_____

_____

_____

_____

_____

_____

_____

_____

Lesson 7 The Writing Process: Letter to the Editor

Revise

After you write a draft, it is a good idea to look closely at what you wrote. You may have made mistakes. Sometimes, what you wrote is not what you meant. It is a hard job, but every writer does it.

Answer the questions below about your draft. If you answer "no" to any of these questions, those areas might need improvement. Feel free to make marks on your draft, so you know what needs more work.

- Did you state your opinion clearly?
- Did you give strong reasons to support your opinion?
- Did you organize those reasons in a logical order, such as least important to most important?
- Did you clearly state what you want your readers to think or do?
- Did you format your business letter correctly?

Think carefully about your audience. With persuasive writing, it is important to aim your arguments at your specific audience. Ask yourself these questions.

- What opinions do my audience already hold about this topic?
- What does my audience already know about this topic?
- What will they need to know in order to understand the issue?
- What emotional appeals might sway the audience in my direction?

It is always a good idea to read your work out loud at the revising stage. You might hear awkward sentences or ideas that do not flow quite right.

Lesson 7 The Writing Process: Letter to the Editor

Write the revision of your first draft here. As you revise, remember to keep your audience in mind.

_____

_____

_____

_____

_____

_____

_____

_____

_____

_____

_____

_____

_____

_____

_____

_____

_____

_____

Lesson 7 The Writing Process: Letter to the Editor

Proofread

Now is the time to correct those last little mistakes. Proofreading is easier if you look for just one kind of error at a time. So, read through for capital letters, and then read for end punctuation. Then, read a third time for spelling. Here is a checklist to use as you proofread your revised letter.

_____ Each sentence begins with a capital letter.
_____ Each sentence ends with the correct punctuation.
_____ Each sentence states a complete thought.
_____ All words are spelled correctly. (If you're not sure, check a dictionary.)
_____ The format of the business letter is correct.

When proofreaders work, they use certain symbols. These symbols will make your job easier, too.

- Three little lines under a letter mean that something should be capitalized.

- Write in a missing end mark like this:⊙ ? !

- Fix incorrect or misspelled words like ~~these~~. *this*

Use these symbols as you proofread your letter. Remember to read your writing out loud, just like you did at the revising stage. Sometimes, you hear mistakes or rough spots that you do not see.

Publish

Now, write a final copy of your letter on a sheet of paper. Write carefully and neatly so that there are no mistakes. If you feel very strongly about the issue, ask permission to submit the letter to the local newspaper.

Chapter 7

Lesson 1 Why Do We Explain?

Explanations, in the form of instructions, are all around. Some of them are simple, such as a door with *push* written on it. You follow the instructions, open the door, and go through. Some of them are not simple. Bicycles, bookshelves, wheelbarrows, and vacuums all come in surprisingly small boxes that are labeled *some assembly required*.

Your teacher might explain how the early settlers of your state applied for statehood. Your parent might explain a math problem.

List some things that someone has explained today.

_____   _____

_____   _____

Think about instructions you have read or used. How many different kinds can you list?

_____ _____ _____

_____ _____ _____

You would write to explain:

- to tell how to make something.

- to tell how something works.

- to tell how to get somewhere.

- to tell why something happened.

What do you know about? Write down a few subjects that you think you could explain clearly.

_____   _____

_____   _____

Lesson 2 Find Causes and Effects

A **cause** is a reason why something happened. An **effect** is a thing that happened as a result of the cause. Here are some examples of causes and effects. Think about the relationship between each cause and effect.

Cause	Effect
The bus is late.	The students are late for class.
The dog ate my homework.	I cannot turn my homework in.
The tree is old and rotten.	The tree was blown down by the wind.

Causes and effects are often used when writing to explain.

The motor moves the lever, which causes the track to move.

When the track moves, the figures appear to dance.

Can you find the causes and effects in the two sentences above? There are three pairs of them. The first one is shown.

Cause	Effect
The motor is on.	The lever moves.
_____	_____
_____	_____

You might also use causes and effects when writing about events that happened in a book.

Jason was lonely, so he put an ad for a friend in the paper. He got so many responses that he didn't have time to do his schoolwork. When he got in trouble, he found out that he already had friends.

Lesson 2 Find Causes and Effects

Find the causes and effects in the paragraph on page 99 about Jason. Write them here. The first one is done for you.

Cause	Effect
Jason is lonely.	He puts an ad in the paper.
_____	_____
_____	_____
_____	_____

Think about a story or book you have read recently. What happened and what did the characters do? Think about the events in terms of causes and effects. What caused this event to happen? What effect did this event have? Write the causes and effects of some important events in the book.

Cause	Effect
_____	_____
_____	_____
_____	_____

Now, use the information from your cause-and-effect chart to write a few sentences about the events of the book. Make sure the cause-and-effect relationships are clear in your sentences. Use the words *so, because, as a result,* and *therefore* to link causes with their effects when you write.

_____

_____

_____

_____

_____

Lesson 3 Relate an Event

James attended his brother's football game on
Friday night. It was an exciting game, and
James is eager to write about it for the school
newspaper, *The Bulldog Press*. His first step was
to list the important facts and events.

1. Bulldogs won the coin toss and chose to receive the kick.
2. Bulldogs ran in the opening kick for a touchdown.
3. Wildcats expected to win the game easily; Bulldogs' touchdown on first play made
   them realize they were going to have to work harder.
4. Wildcats played fiercely, and several Bulldogs were injured.
5. Injuries caused Bulldogs to play even harder; held Wildcats away from end zone.
6. Final score, 7–0, with Bulldogs on top.

James's list included some causes and their effects. They help explain what
happened and why. Here is one set of causes and effects from the first
two items on the list.

Cause: Bulldogs chose to receive
     the opening kick

Effect: Bulldogs caught kick and
     scored on opening play

Here is part of James's article about the game. Look for words that signal
cause-and-effect relationships, such as *so, because, as a result*, and
therefore. Circle each one you find.

> The Bulldogs' early touchdown was a wake-up call for the Wildcats, so their
> defense really put on the steam to stop the Bulldogs from scoring again. As a result,
> several Bulldogs were injured during the first half.
> Because of the injuries, the rest of the Bulldogs rallied during the second half.
> They didn't allow the Wildcats anywhere near the end zone. As a result, the score
> stayed at 7–0, and the Wildcats returned home with their first loss of the season.

Lesson 3 Relate an Event

Think about the causes and effects in your own life. What happened yesterday? What did you do? List some of yesterday's events in order. Draw arrows to show any cause-and-effect relationship among events.

1. _____

2. _____

3. _____

4. _____

5. _____

Now, practice writing about causes and effects. Write a paragraph about yesterday, using the list you made above. Remember to use *so, because, as a result,* or *therefore* to connect the cause-and-effect relationships.

_____

_____

_____

_____

_____

_____

_____

_____

_____

_____

NAME _____

Lesson 4 Review Your Verbs

Verbs that tell about an action that is happening now are **present tense** verbs. Circle the verb in each sentence.

Lights flash.

Emergency vehicles race to the site of the crash.

Verbs that tell about an action that already happened are **past tense** verbs. Circle the verbs.

Sirens blared.

Rescue workers dashed toward the ditch.

Most past tense verbs are formed by adding **d** or **ed** to the present tense form of the word. For example, *blare* becomes *blared* and *dash* becomes *dashed*. Verbs that form the past tense in this way are called **regular verbs**.

Circle the regular verb in each sentence. Then, write the past tense form of that verb by adding **d** or **ed**.

Drivers slow their cars. _____

People watch out their windows. _____

Children cover their ears. _____

Two dogs howl at the noise. _____

Two older people close their windows. _____

They all wonder what is happening. _____

Lesson 4 Review Your Verbs

Some verbs are called **irregular verbs**, meaning that their past tense is not formed by adding **d** or **ed**. Here are examples of the present and past forms of some irregular verbs:

Present	→	**Past**
sit	→	sat
think	→	thought
fall	→	fell
tear	→	tore
bite	→	bit

As you can see, there is no rule or pattern. Each irregular verb is different, and you must memorize each one. If you are unsure about the past tense of a verb, look up the present tense form in a dictionary.

Circle the verb in each sentence. Then, write the irregular past tense form of that verb. Use a dictionary if needed.

Collin drives all day. _____

He begins to get tired. _____

He drinks water to stay alert. _____

Sometimes, he eats a snack. _____

After lunch, he takes a nap. _____

Then, he runs around the car for exercise. _____

Now, write two sentences about riding in a car. Use verbs in the past tense. You may use regular or irregular verbs. Label the regular verbs with an **R** and the irregular verbs with an **I**.

_____

_____

Lesson 5 Add a Picture

When writing to explain, you tell how to do something, how to get somewhere, or how something works. Many types of explanations are made more clear with the addition of a picture, map, graph, or diagram. Can you imagine putting together a bicycle without having pictures to go along with the instructions? Here is what they might look like without illustrations:

> Find the bolt with the hexagonal head that measures $\frac{3}{8}$" across and is $\frac{9}{16}$" long. Then, find the washer whose opening is $\frac{1}{4}$". Fit the washer onto the bolt. Then, put the bolt into the hole in the round end of the blue bracket that fits onto the seat support.

However, if the instructions have a complete diagram, including labeled pictures of each part, the instructions might look like this:

> Fit washer W2 onto bolt B4. Place in opening O44.

Sometimes, a picture shows a great deal of information, which means the writer does not have to work so hard to explain something. Sometimes, a picture shows information better than a writer could explain it. Here is an example:

Hardin Elementary has a traffic problem before and after school. The cars get in a terrible jam, and the principal is worried about the safety of the students. The large bar on the graph labeled "Students who are dropped off by parents" clearly shows why the problem exists.

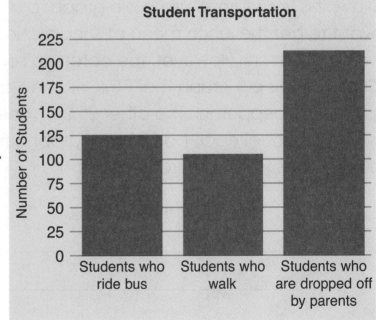

Lesson 5 Add a Picture

The principal of Hardin Elementary asked the city to widen the street so that there will be a safe drop-off point for students. The City Council, however, said it has no money for this project. Here is part of the letter the council wrote to the principal.

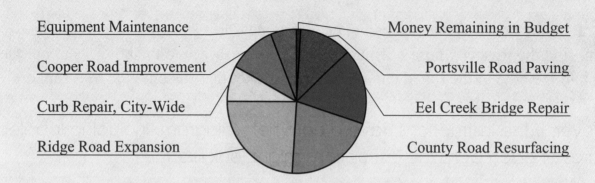

The Council regrets that funds for street improvement are not available. A number of street projects have already been completed this year, and there is no budget for additional projects.

Equipment Maintenance

Cooper Road Improvement

Curb Repair, City-Wide

Ridge Road Expansion

Money Remaining in Budget

Portsville Road Paving

Eel Creek Bridge Repair

County Road Resurfacing

The City Council's graph shows, at a glance, that they do not have much money left in the budget. The "picture" of the budget is much more effective and easier to understand than a long, wordy explanation of how and where the money was spent.

Now, it is your turn to use a pie graph to make a point. Imagine that you want to get the lunch menu at school changed. Most students prefer pizza with pepperoni. However, the cafeteria serves only pizza with sausage. Show on this pie graph that 75%, or three-quarters, of the students prefer pizza with pepperoni. The other 25%, or one-quarter, prefer pizza with sausage. Label each part of your graph. Then, write a sentence that summarizes what the graph shows.

_____

_____

Lesson 6 Give Me Directions

You walk into school and see an unfamiliar student standing just inside the door. He is obviously new and lost. He asks you how to get to the gym. Can you give clear directions to help the new student find the way?

Directions, just like how-to instructions, need to be in order. In addition, they need to tell *where*. Here are some words to help you write clear directions.

Direction Words	Position Words	Time-Order Words
left	over	first
right	under	second
up	past	then
down	beyond	next
north	before	after that
west	above	finally
	beside	

Here are directions to get to the gym at Philippe's school. Notice how Philippe uses some of the words from the lists above. Circle them when you find them.

_____ First, go down this blue hallway. Just before you get to the double glass doors, turn right. Go past the nurse's office. Just beyond the trophy case, turn left and you will see the big gym doors.

Lesson 6 Give Me Directions

Write directions that tell how to get from your classroom to the gym.

_____

_____

_____

_____

_____

_____

There is an island with a hidden treasure. You know where the treasure is, but you want to write directions to make sure you remember. What paths must you follow? How do you know where to turn? Make a sketch that shows the island, the location of the treasure, and any helpful landmarks, if you want. Then, write directions to the treasure to help you remember.

_____

_____

_____

_____

_____

_____

_____

Lesson 7 The Writing Process: How-To Instructions

Use the writing process to explain to someone else how to do something.

Prewrite

Think about things that you know how to do. You probably know how to play various games or how to put together a good snack, Maybe you know how to fold paper to make an envelope or how to make a bird feeder out of a soft drink bottle. Write down some things that you know how to do.

_____   _____

_____   _____

_____   _____

Look over your list and imagine explaining how to do each thing. Pick a topic and write down everything you can think of about it. Add to this idea web as needed.

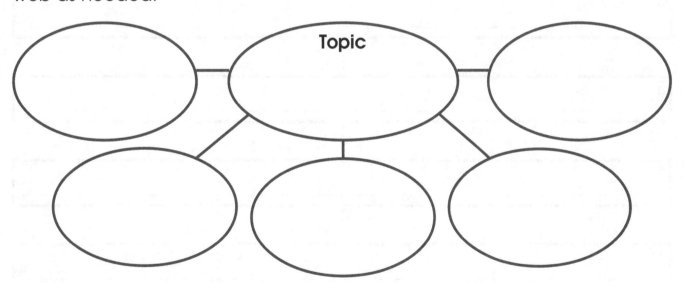

Are you comfortable with your topic? If not, go back to your list and choose another. Explore it with an idea web on a separate sheet of paper. Remember to think about the details that someone else will need to know about the process.

Lesson 7 The Writing Process: How-To Instructions

Now, it is time to focus on putting ideas in order. Think about the process you are about to explain. Assume that your audience has never done this before, so you need to start at the very beginning. Use the sequence chart to list the important steps in your explanation. Be sure to put them in the correct order.

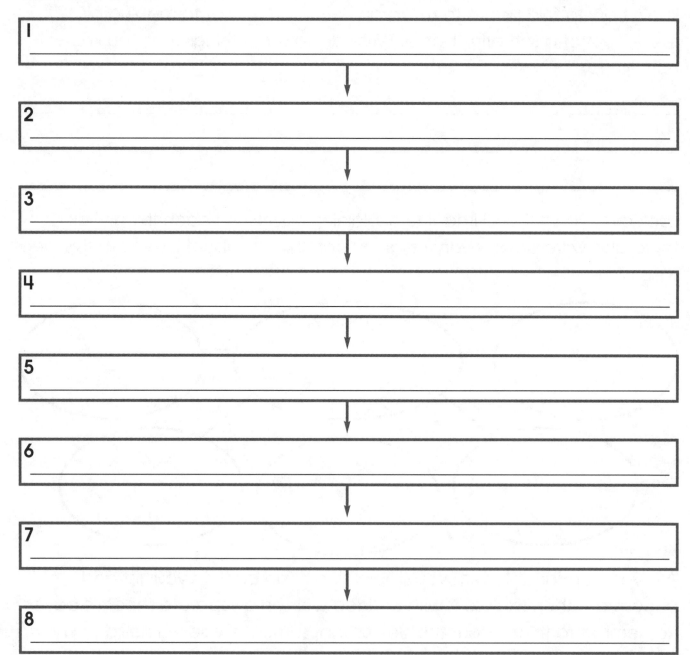

1 _____

2 _____

3 _____

4 _____

5 _____

6 _____

7 _____

8 _____

Lesson 7 The Writing Process: How-To Instructions

Draft

Now, write your first draft of your instructions. Use your sequence chart to help you. As you write, do not worry about misspelling words or getting everything perfect. Just get your ideas down in sentences and in order.

_____

_____

_____

_____

_____

_____

_____

_____

_____

_____

_____

_____

_____

_____

_____

_____

Lesson 7 The Writing Process: How-To Instructions

Revise

Whenever you write, you work hard to write well. It is very hard to go back and ask yourself, "How can I make this better?" But that is what every writer must do. Answer the questions below about your draft. If you answer "no" to any of these questions, those are the areas that might need improvement. Feel free to make marks on your draft, so you know what needs more work.

> - Did you explain how to do something from beginning to end?
> - Did you include all of the steps in order?
> - Did you include time-order words to make the sequence clear?
> - Did you use direction, position, and/or time-order words to make your details clear?
> - Did you use good describing words so your readers can "see" what they are supposed to do?
> - Did you keep your audience in mind by asking yourself what they might already know or what they need to know?
> - Did you include a heading or title so readers know what they are reading about?

Now, review how to form past tense verbs.

- Most verbs are regular verbs. Form the past tense by adding **d** or **ed** to the present tense form. Here are some examples of regular verbs:

  dance   ➜   dance**d**   chatter   ➜   chatter**ed**

- Some verbs are irregular. Their past tense forms do not follow a pattern. Here are some commonly used irregular verbs:

run	➜	ran	tell	➜	told
bring	➜	brought	say	➜	said

On your draft, circle any past tense verbs that you are not sure about.

Lesson 7 The Writing Process: How-To Instructions

Write a revision of your first draft. As you revise, remember to think about important details that make your steps clear.

_____

_____

_____

_____

_____

_____

_____

_____

_____

_____

_____

_____

_____

_____

_____

_____

Lesson 7 The Writing Process: How-To Instructions

Proofread

Now, it is the time to correct those last little mistakes. Proofreading is easier if you look for just one kind of error at a time. So, read through once for capital letters. Read again for end punctuation. Read a third time for spelling. Here is a checklist to use as you proofread your instructions.

____ Each sentence begins with a capital letter.

____ Each sentence ends with the correct punctuation.

____ Each sentence states a complete thought.

____ All words are spelled correctly. (If you are not sure, check a dictionary.)

When proofreaders work, they use certain symbols. Using these symbols makes their job easier. They will make your job easier, too.

- three little lines under a letter mean that something should be capitalized.

- Write in a missing end mark like this: ⊙ ? !

- "Please add a comma and quotation marks" she said.

- Fix incorrect or misspelled words like these.

Use these symbols as you proofread your instructions. Remember to read your writing out loud, even if there is no one to listen. Sometimes when reading, you can hear mistakes or rough spots that you did not see.

Lesson 7 The Writing Process: How-To Instructions

Publish

Write your final copy. Write carefully and neatly so that there are no mistakes. If you wish, include a graph, chart, or diagram to enhance your instructions and to make them clearer. Read your instructions out loud or give a demonstration in front of an audience.

_____

_____

_____

_____

_____

_____

_____

_____

_____

_____

_____

_____

_____

_____

_____

Chapter 8

NAME _____

When you write a report for school, you are writing to inform. When writing to inform, you present information about a topic.

Carmen wrote a report about autumn leaves.

Carmen M.

Autumn Leaves

The leaves on the trees have worked hard all summer. They were busy using carbon dioxide and water to make food, called *glucose*, for the trees. This process of making food is called *photosynthesis*, which means putting together with light. The chemical that makes photosynthesis possible is chlorophyll. Chlorophyll is what gives plants their green color.

As the autumn days get shorter, there is less light. As a result, less photosynthesis takes place, so the tree produces less and less chlorophyll. This causes the green color to fade from the leaves.

The yellow and orange colors are the result of other chemicals in the leaves. They were there all along, but were covered up by the chlorophyll. Red leaves, like those on a sugar maple, are the result of glucose that is trapped in the leaves after photosynthesis stops.

The changing leaf color that occurs each fall is a simple chemical process that is just one part of the life cycle of a tree.

Lesson 1 Why and How Do We Inform?

Here are the features of informational writing:

- It gives important information about a topic.
- It presents a main idea, which is supported with facts.
- It may include information from several different sources.
- It draws a conclusion based on the information presented.
- It is organized in a logical way. Transition words are used to connect ideas.

Why do people write to inform?

At school, you write book reports and reports about bats, George Washington, and volcanoes. Many adults use informational writing at work. They might write a company report, which explains how business is going and whether the company is successful or not. They might write about a new product and how it will save people money or make something easier. Informational writing is also used in letters. In a friendly letter, you might report on a recent school activity. In a business letter, you might inform a magazine publisher, for example, that your address has changed.

Who reads informational writing?

Everyone does. When you write at school, your teacher and your classmates are usually your audience. Remember to think about your audience as you write. What might they already know about the topic? What might they need or want to know?

What can informational writing be about?

You can write to inform about anything that involves facts. Informational writing often involves doing research, then telling or reporting what you know or what you have learned.

Lesson 1 Why and How Do We Inform?

When writing to inform, use transition words to connect ideas. The transition words help readers understand the connections. Here are some common transition words:

and	consequently
also	for example
as a result	however
at the same time	therefore
because	thus
before long	when
but	

Read Carmen's report on page 116 again. Find the transition words that Carmen used. Circle them.

It is always a good idea to choose a topic in which you are interested. Answer these questions to help you think of possible topics.

What are some wild animals that interest you?

_____ _____ _____

_____ _____ _____

What are some places in the world that interest you or that you would like to visit?

_____ _____ _____

_____ _____ _____

Who are some interesting people you have read about? They might be authors, scientists, soldiers, presidents, pilots, or racecar drivers.

_____ _____ _____

_____ _____ _____

Lesson 2 Facts, Opinions, and Bias

Facts can be proven to be true. Opinions are judgments that people make. Do you know what bias is?

Bias is an unfair opinion that a writer gives to a topic. Some writers may do it by accident. Perhaps they have such strong views that they do not realize they are presenting only one point of view or only a portion of the facts. Other writers bias their work on purpose in order to present their own views and to persuade others to believe as they do.

Can you find the bias—the unfair slant—in this portion of a travel article?

> Florida is a beautiful state, but I would never want to be there in summer. The heat and humidity would drain me of all energy. In winter, however, it is delightful. Imagine eating Thanksgiving dinner on a sun-drenched patio. Think of strolling under palm trees on New Year's Eve. Florida has plenty to offer for any traveler.

The writer's views come out loud and clear. The writer says nice things about Florida and encourages people to travel, but during only one season. The writer forgets that some people might like hot and humid weather.

It is important for readers to recognize bias when they see it. Ads often include bias, which is one method of persuasion. News stories might contain bias, which could lead readers to misunderstand an issue or to vote for a different candidate, for example. So, it is important to think about what is fact, what is opinion, and to ask whether all sides of an issue are being fairly presented. As a writer, you should ask the same questions.

Lesson 2 Facts, Opinions, and Bias

Imagine that John Smith and Bill Jones are running for president. You went to school with John Smith, and you remember that he was always very fair. Bill Jones, on the other hand, used to work for the same company as you do. You never really got along with him. He was a hard worker, however, and seemed really smart. Compare the two candidates in a paragraph. Show bias in the paragraph by favoring John Smith.

_____

_____

_____

_____

_____

Now, write a paragraph in which you fairly present the strong points of both candidates. Make up details as needed. Remember, you may express your opinion (about favoring John Smith), but you should present information about both candidates in a fair and even manner.

_____

_____

_____

_____

_____

_____

Lesson 3 The Writing Process: Biography

A biography is an account of a real person's life written by another person. A good biography contains only true information about the person or subject. Biographers may express their opinions, but they must be careful not to bias their writing. For example, writing about the accomplishments of Benjamin Franklin would be only half the story. Like any scientist, he had many failures that affected the course of his life as well as his later successes. A good biographer should present the whole picture and let the reader form his or her own opinion of the subject.

Use the writing process to plan and write a biography.

Prewrite

Look back at the final question on page 118. What names did you list? Which of those people seems most interesting? Choose one and begin to explore that person by answering the questions below.

Biography subject: _____

What is this person known for? _____

Why does this person seem interesting to you? _____

_____

If you are comfortable with this subject, conduct some research and create a time line of the person's life. Write the person's birth date at the left end of the line. Write the year the person died (or present year, if that person is alive) at the right end. Fill in important events in order along the time line.

├───┤

Lesson 3 The Writing Process: Biography

Now, it is time to focus on putting ideas in order. Think about your subject's life. Many biographers break up a subject's life into phases. Use the chart on this page to record important information about the early, middle, and late stages of your subject's life. Remember to present an unbiased set of facts.

Name of Subject: _____

Early Life
_____
_____
_____

Middle Life
_____
_____
_____

Late Life
_____
_____
_____

Accomplishments or Contributions
_____
_____
_____

Lesson 3 The Writing Process: Biography

Draft

Write a first draft of your biography. Keep your notes and the chart on page 122 nearby as you write. Write your draft on this page. Continue on another sheet of paper if you need to. As you write, don't worry about misspelling words or getting everything perfect. Just write your ideas down in sentences and in time-order.

_____

_____

_____

_____

_____

_____

_____

_____

_____

_____

_____

_____

_____

_____

Lesson 3 The Writing Process: Biography

Revise

Every writer can improve his or her work. Pick up your paper and read it with fresh eyes. Keep in mind that most writers feel that revising is much more difficult than writing the first draft.

Answer the questions below about your draft. If you answer "no" to any of these questions, those are the areas that might need improvement. Feel free to make marks on your draft so you know what needs more work.

- Did you present information clearly and in a logical order?
- Does each paragraph consist of a main idea supported by facts?
- Did you include transition words to connect ideas?
- Did you begin with a sentence that will interest your readers?
- Did you use information from several different sources?
- Did you draw a conclusion, based on the information presented?
- Did you keep your audience in mind by asking yourself what they might already know or what they need to know?
- Did you present a fair or balanced view of the subject?

Here are a few pointers about making your biography interesting to read.

- Do not begin with a sentence like this: *Andrew Carnegie was born on November 25, 1835.* It is very logical but not very interesting. Instead, you might begin with: *No one could run a business or make money like Andrew Carnegie.*

- Do not end your biography with a sentence like this: *Andrew Carnegie died on August 11, 1919.* Again, it is logical but not very interesting. Instead, write a sentence that somehow summarizes the subject or his or her importance. Here is an example: *By giving away more than $350 million during his lifetime, Carnegie earned his place as one of America's greatest philanthropists.*

Lesson 3 The Writing Process: Biography

Write a revision of your draft below. As you revise, pay special attention to your opening and closing sentences.

_____

_____

_____

_____

_____

_____

_____

_____

_____

_____

_____

_____

_____

_____

_____

_____

_____

_____

Lesson 3 The Writing Process: Biography

Proofread

Now is the time to correct those last little mistakes. Proofreading is easier if you look for just one kind of error at a time. Read through once for capital letters. Read again for end punctuation. Read a third time for spelling. Use this checklist as you proofread your biography.

_____ Each sentence begins with a capital letter.

_____ Each sentence ends with the correct punctuation.

_____ Each sentence states a complete thought.

_____ All proper nouns begin with capital letters.

_____ All words are spelled correctly. (If you are not sure, check a dictionary.)

When proofreaders work, they use certain symbols. Using these symbols makes their job easier. They will make your job easier, too.

- three little lines under a letter mean that something should be capitalized.

- Write in a missing end mark like this: ⊙ ? !

- "Please add a comma and quotation marks" she said.

- Fix incorect or misspelled words like these.

Use these symbols as you proofread your biography. Remember to read your writing out loud. Sometimes, you can hear mistakes or rough spots that you did not see when writing.

Lesson 3 The Writing Process: Biography

Publish

Write your final copy below carefully and neatly so that there are no mistakes. Make a cover that includes a drawing or photocopied picture of your subject. Read your biography out loud to your class or family.

_____

_____

_____

_____

_____

_____

_____

_____

_____

_____

_____

_____

_____

_____

_____

Writer's Handbook

Writing Basics

Sentences are a writer's building blocks. To be a good writer, one must first be a good sentence writer. A sentence always begins with a capital letter.

He walked around the block.

A sentence must always tell a complete thought. It has a subject and a predicate.

Complete Sentence: He lives around the corner.
Incomplete Sentence: The block where he lives.

A sentence always ends with an end mark. There are three kinds of end marks. A sentence that tells something ends with a period.

He walked around the block.

A sentence that asks something ends with a question mark.

Did he walk around the block**?**

A sentence that shows excitement or fear ends with an exclamation point.

He ran all the way around the block**!**

Punctuation can be a writer's road map.

End marks on sentences show whether a sentence is a statement, a question, or an exclamation.

Commas help keep ideas clear.

In a list or series: I saw sea stars, crabs, and seals at the beach.
In a compound sentence: I wanted a closer look, but the crab crawled away.
After an introductory phrase or clause: Later that day, a storm blew up.
To separate a speech tag: I called to Mom, "It's really getting windy!"
                               "I hope it doesn't rain," she said.

Quotation marks show the exact words that a speaker says. Quotation marks enclose the speaker's words and the punctuation marks that go with the words.

"Does it matter?" Neil remarked. "We're already wet."
"I'd rather be wet from below than from above," said Dad.
"Be careful!" Mom yelled. "Those waves are getting big!"

Writer's Handbook

The Writing Process

When writers write, they take certain steps. Those steps make up the writing process.

Step 1: Prewrite

First, writers choose a topic. Then, they collect and organize ideas or information. They might write their ideas in a list or make a chart and begin to put their ideas in some kind of order.

Mariko is going to write about her neighborhood. She put her ideas in a web.

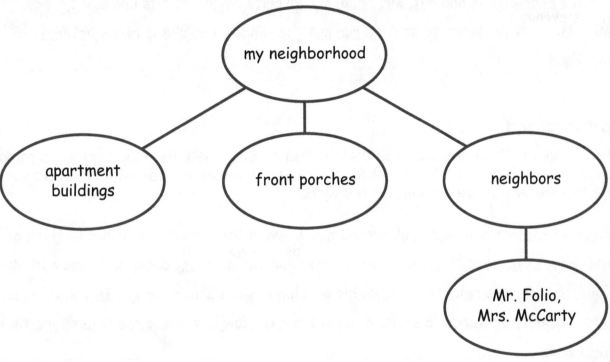

Step 2: Draft

Next, writers put their ideas on paper in a first draft. Writers know that there might be mistakes in this first draft. That's okay. Here is Mariko's first draft.

> Brick apartment houses are all around me. I live in tallest one. Across the street is the shortest. I like to think of the windows as eyes. and the front porches are the mouths People go in and out. Mr. Folio, my favorite neighbor, sits and sings songs. Mrs. McCarty pretends to shake a rug out the window but she is really listening to Mr. Folio.

Writer's Handbook

Step 3: Revise

Then, writers change or fix their first draft. They might decide to move ideas around, add information, or take out words or sentences that don't belong. Here are Mariko's changes.

> Brick apartment houses are all around me. I live in the tallest one. ~~Across the street~~ ~~is the shortest.~~ I like to think of the windows as eyes, and the front porches are the mouths People go in and out. Mr. Folio, my favorite neighbor, sits on his porch and sings Italian songs. In the evening, Mrs. McCarty pretends to shake a rug out the window but she is really listening to Mr. Folio.

Step 4: Proofread

Writers usually write a new copy so their writing is neat. Then, they look again to make sure everything is correct. They look for mistakes in their sentences. Mariko found several more mistakes when she proofread her work.

> Brick apartment houses are all around me. I live in the tallest one. I like to think of the windows as eyes and the front porches are the mouths as People go in and out. Mr. Folio, my favorite neighbor, sits on his porch and sings Italian songs. In the evening, Mrs. McCarty pretends to shake a rug out the window but she is really listening to Mr. Folio.

Step 5: Publish

Finally, writers make a final copy that has no mistakes. They might choose to add pictures and create a book. Then, they are ready to publish their writing. They might choose to read their writing out loud or have a friend read it.

Writer's Handbook

Personal Narrative

In a personal narrative, a writer writes about something she has done or seen. It might tell about something funny, sad, or unusual. A personal narrative can be about anything, as long as the writer is telling about one of his or her own experiences. Here is the final version of Mariko's paragraph about her neighborhood.

Describing words help readers "see" or "hear" what is happening.	Brick apartment houses are all around me. I live in the tallest one. I like to think of the windows as eyes and front porches as mouths. People go in and out. Mr. Folio, my favorite neighbor, sits on his porch and sings Italian songs. In the evening, Mrs. McCarty pretends to shake a rug out the window, but she is really listening to Mr. Folio.	The words *me* and *I* show that the writer is part of the action.
A time word tells when something happens.		The writer stayed on topic. All of the sentences give information about Mariko's neighborhood.

Stories

Writers write about made-up things. They might write about people or animals. The story might seem real, or it might seem fantastic, or unreal. Here is a story that Mariko wrote. It has both human and animal characters in it. The animals speak, so Mariko's story is not realistic.

The story has a beginning, a middle, and an end.	**In the Neighborhood**	The first paragraph establishes the setting.
Sensory words help readers visualize what is happening.	It is nearly sunrise, and the neighborhood is waking up. Windows glow where the early birds prepare breakfast. Bacon sizzles in the Hooper kitchen, and the smell draws a hungry crowd. In the corner, eight furry paws scramble through the crack between the wall and the baseboard. They pause at the corner of the wastebasket, then scamper to the refrigerator. Blue fuzzy slippers come quickly forward and stamp on the floor. "Go away, you critters!" The critters huddle deeper in the darkness. Four black eyes watch for crumbs to fall. Two long tails twitch with excitement.	Time and order words keep ideas in order.
The story includes dialogue, or conversation among characters.	Mrs. Hooper's slippers scuff across the floor. "It's ready!" she calls upstairs. In a moment, Mr. Hooper's heavy work boots thump down the stairs. *Scuff-thump*, *Scuff-thump*, the people go into the other room. "Now, it's our turn," smiles Velvet. Her brother Flannel nods and shrugs. "It's a dirty job, but someone has to do it." And he and his sister go to work, clearing the floor of crumbs.	This story is written in third-person point of view. So, words such as *he*, *she*, *her*, *his*, and *they* refer to the characters.

Writer's Handbook

Descriptive Writing

When writers describe, they might tell about an object, a place, or an event. They use sensory words so that readers can see, hear, smell, feel, or taste whatever is being described. In this example of descriptive writing, Mariko compared her old bedroom with her new bedroom.

> The writer uses the whole-to-whole comparison method. She describes one whole room in the first paragraph, and the other room in the second paragraph.

> My bedroom in our old apartment was green. It was a nice grassy green, and it always made me think of a forest. My bed was in the left corner, between the two windows. The wall straight ahead was almost all shelves, where I kept my turtle collection, my books, and all my other stuff. My yellow beanbag chair and the closet were on the right side of the room.
>
> My new bedroom is blue. I like to think of it as sky blue. On the left side of the room is one big window. I put my beanbag chair right beside the window. Straight ahead is my bed. On the right is a built-in bookshelf and the closet door.

> Sensory details help readers visualize the scene.

> The writer organizes details from side to side. She first tells what is on the left, then straight ahead, then on the right.

Informational Writing

When writers write to inform, they present information about a topic. Informational writing is nonfiction. It is not made up; it contains facts.

Mariko interviewed her neighbor, Mr. Folio. Then, she wrote about what she learned. Here is one of her paragraphs.

> Mariko states her main idea in a topic sentence. It is the first sentence of the paragraph.

> Transition words connect ideas.

> My neighbor, Mr. Folio, has lived in the same apartment building all his life. His parents and his grandparents lived there, too. In fact, his grandparents were the first people to move into the building in 1921. He remembers his grandmother telling about how new and shiny the doorknobs and the stair railings were. Mr. Folio's grandparents lived on the top floor because his grandfather liked the view. Later his parents lived on the fourth floor because that was what was available at the time. Now Mr. Folio lives on the first floor. He says he likes to see what is going on in the neighborhood.

> These sentences contain details that support the main idea.

Writer's Handbook

Explanatory (or How-to) Writing

Writers explain how to do things. They might write about how to play a game, create an art project, or follow a recipe. Mariko has written instructions for a marble game that she plays with her sister.

| The steps are all in order, starting with the items needed to play the game. | **Mariko's Marbles**
First, you need 20 small marbles, two shooter marbles, and someone to play with. Choose a square of sidewalk that doesn't have very many cracks or bumps in it. Roll the small marbles onto the square. Then, players take turns using their shooters to try to knock marbles out of the square. Each player gets two tries per turn. Players may knock out only one marble at a time. If a player knocks out more than one marble, the player must put back all of her knocked-out marbles. Finally, when all 20 marbles have been knocked out of the square, the player with the most marbles is the winner. | Clear words help readers understand the instructions. |
| Order words help readers keep the steps in order. | | |

Persuasive Writing

In persuasive writing, writers try to make readers think, feel, or act in a certain way. Persuasive writing shows up in newspaper and magazine articles, letters to the editor, business letters, and in advertisements, of course. Mariko's mom has written a letter to the editor of the local newspaper.

| The writer begins by stating some opinions. | Dear Editor:
    I used to be proud of my neighborhood. The streets used to look nice, and people cared about keeping them that way. Now, however, the sidewalks on 41st Street are terribly cracked and broken, and the city has no plans to fix them. In some places, it is not even safe to walk. The older people in the neighborhood have to walk in the street to get to the grocery store. Can't the city repair the sidewalks? It would feel good to be proud and safe in my neighborhood again.
                                        F. Torunaga | The writer states some facts to lend support to her opinions. |
| The writer uses an emotional appeal to persuade readers to agree with her. | | The writer includes a specific request for action. |

Writer's Handbook

Friendly Letters

Writers write friendly letters to people they know. They might share news or ideas or request information. A friendly letter has five parts: the date, the greeting, the body, the closing, and the signature. Here is a letter Mariko wrote to her grandfather.

Each word in the greeting begins with a capital letter.

There is always a comma after the person's name.

The date is in the upper, right corner.

The body of the letter gives information.

Only the first word of the closing begins with a capital letter. There is always a comma after the closing.

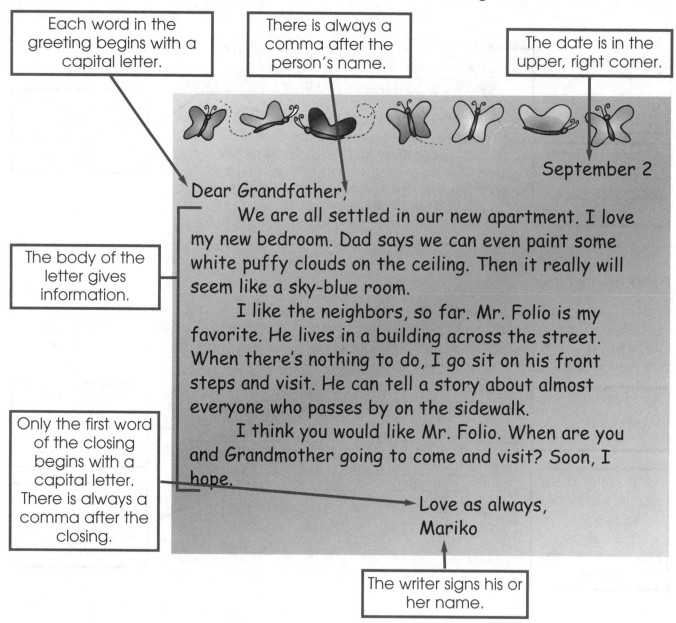

September 2

Dear Grandfather,

We are all settled in our new apartment. I love my new bedroom. Dad says we can even paint some white puffy clouds on the ceiling. Then it really will seem like a sky-blue room.

I like the neighbors, so far. Mr. Folio is my favorite. He lives in a building across the street. When there's nothing to do, I go sit on his front steps and visit. He can tell a story about almost everyone who passes by on the sidewalk.

I think you would like Mr. Folio. When are you and Grandmother going to come and visit? Soon, I hope.

Love as always,
Mariko

The writer signs his or her name.

Writer's Handbook

Business Letters

Writers write business letters to people or organizations with whom they are not familiar. Business letters usually involve a complaint or a request for information. Mariko needs information for a school report. She wrote a business letter to request information.

The heading includes the sender's address and the date.

764 41st Street
Indianapolis, IN 46208
October 5, 2007

The inside address is the name and address of the recipient.

Monroe County Historical Society
202 E. 6th Street
Bloomington, IN 47402

Dear Monroe County Historical Society:

The greeting is followed by a colon.

The text of the letter is the body.

My class is studying state history this year. Each of us has chosen a county to study. I chose Monroe County because my grandparents live there.

On your Web site, I saw that you have a free pamphlet titled "Monroe County: Through the Years." Please send me one copy of that brochure. I have included an envelope with postage.

Thank you for your help with my report.

Sincerely,

Mariko Torunaga

Mariko Torunaga

The sender always includes a signature.

The closing is followed by a comma.

Answer Key

Chapter 1

Lesson 1

Page 5
Garden: seed packet, shovel, soil, plant
Tools: hammer, pliers, screwdriver, saw
Electrical: light bulb, cord, light switch, lamp

Page 6
Possible categories and lists:
Laundry: 3 dirty socks, 1 dirty pair of jeans, 1 shirt with a spot on it
Toys: a set of magnets, 2 horse figurines, a box of modeling clay
Bookshelf items: a photo album, 4 books, a journal

Lesson 2

Page 7
Underlined sentence: This year's play is "Little Red Riding Hood."
Main idea: Bill fell on an icy patch.

Page 8
Main ideas will vary.
Underlined main idea: Kira played with her food.

Page 9
Main idea: Volcanoes come in different shapes.
Paragraphs will vary.

Lesson 3

Page 10
Details will vary.

Page 11
Details will vary.
Paragraphs will vary.

Lesson 4

Page 12
Topic sentence: I never dreamed that the beach would be so great.
Topic sentence: I hate rainy days.

Page 13
Topic sentences:
A spring rain is a marvelous thing.
All rain is not the same.
Paragraphs will vary.

Lesson 5

Page 14
There is a dolphin having a picnic on the grass.
Main ideas will vary.

Page 15
Paragraph 1
Topic sentence: Mr. Hansen is my favorite teacher of all time.
Details will vary.
Off-topic sentence: Birds have hollow bones.
Paragraph 2
Topic sentence: The time line that goes around our classroom helps us keep historical events in order.
Details will vary.
Off-topic sentence: They carried long spears and wore helmets.

Lesson 6

Page 16
Problems in paragraph:
First line of paragraph is not indented.
"They did not ride bikes" is off topic.
"Some surrounded by miles of earthen walls" is not a complete sentence.

Page 17
Paragraphs will vary.

Answer Key

Chapter 2

Lesson 1

Page 18
Purposes for Writing (Some answers may vary.)
letter to editor: to persuade, to inform
story: to entertain
article: to inform
instructions: to explain

Lesson 2

Page 19
Writing Topics (possible matches)
friend or classmate: your last soccer game, instructions for a computer game, an account of a field trip
parent: instructions for a computer game, an account of a field trip
grandparent: your last soccer game, an account of a field trip
teacher: a report on school lunches, a book report
principal: a report on school lunches

Lesson 3

Page 20
Posters will vary.

Page 21
Announcements will vary.

Lesson 4

Page 23
Letters will vary.

Lesson 5

Page 24
Ideas will vary.

Page 25
Instructions will vary.

Lesson 6

Page 26
Answers will vary.

Page 27
Advertisements will vary.

Lesson 7

Page 29
Order of steps shown:
Step 4: Proofread
Step 2: Draft
Step 3: Revise
Step 1: Prewrite
Step 5: Publish

Lesson 8

Page 30
Topics will vary.

Page 31
Topic sentences and supporting ideas will vary.
Drafts will vary.

Page 32
Revisions will vary.

Page 33
Published opinion statements will vary.

Answer Key

Chapter 3

Lesson 1

Page 35
Ideas will vary.

Lesson 2

Page 36
Circle "after," "as soon as," and "after."
Sentences will vary.

Page 37
Sentences will vary.

Lesson 3

Page 38
Sentences will vary.

Page 39
Sentences will vary.

Lesson 4

Page 40
Entries in idea webs will vary.

Page 41
Sequence charts will vary.

Page 42
Drafts will vary.

Page 44
Revisions will vary.

Answer Key

Chapter 4

Lesson 1
Page 46
Details will vary.

Page 47
Descriptions will vary.

Lesson 2
Page 48
Sentences will vary.

Page 49
Sentences will vary.

Lesson 3
Page 50
Descriptions will vary.

Page 51
Descriptions will vary.

Lesson 4
Page 52
Possible details in Venn diagram:
Apple: hard, shiny
Both: red, round
Playground Ball: soft, bouncy, dull

Page 53
Comparisons and sentences will vary.

Lesson 5
Page 54
Joe is sloppier than Dexter.
Dexter is neater than Joe.
Do you think Joe's clothes are more
   comfortable than Dexter's?

Page 55
Students' sentences should contain the
   words biggest, smallest, most gigantic,
   and wrinkliest.

Lesson 6
Page 56
Details in Venn diagrams will vary.

Page 57
Paragraphs will vary.

Lesson 7
Page 58
Lists and details in idea webs will vary.

Page 59
Organized details and drafts will vary.

Page 60
Revisions will vary.

Page 61
Final descriptive paragraphs will vary.

Answer Key

Chapter 5

Lesson 1

Page 63
Characters: Charlie, Charlotte
Setting: woods
Words from the story: "dry creek bed," "rock," "burrow"
Problem: A dog appears near the chipmunks
Charlie is a bold chipmunk. His words show that he is very sure of himself.
Sense words: "leaves crackle," "nervously," "scampered," "the sun was high in the sky," "dry creek bed," "loud crackling sound," "squeaked," "large brown head and pointy ears"

Lesson 2

Page 64
"That sounds like a good idea," responded Taylor.
Eve asked, "What is a read-a-thon?"
"Dalton, why don't you tell everyone?" said Taylor.

Page 65
Dialogue will vary.

Lesson 3

Page 66
Responses will vary.

Page 67
Responses will vary.

Lesson 4

Page 68
Responses will vary.

Page 69
Responses will vary.

Lesson 5

Page 71
Responses will vary.

Lesson 6

Page 72
Responses will vary.

Page 73
Responses will vary.

Lesson 7

Page 74
Entries in idea webs will vary.

Page 75
Story maps will vary.

Page 76
Drafts will vary.

Page 78
Revisions will vary.

Answer Key

Chapter 6

Lesson 1
Page 81
Persuasive writing will vary.

Lesson 2
Page 82
Facts: Some people in community don't have enough to eat. The food pantry is on Carver Street. It is run by volunteers. Pantry had a yard sale on Saturday.
Opinions: "I think it's shameful..." "Pantry shouldn't have to solve that problem all by itself." "City should help solve problem." "We shouldn't have to be holding yard sales..."

Page 83
Circled opinion words in letter to the editor on page 82: I think, shouldn't, should, shouldn't
Opinion statements will vary.

Lesson 3
Page 84
Slogans will vary.

Page 85
Slogans and responses will vary.

Lesson 4
Page 87
(left column) passive
(right column) active
Jae
Dandelions
X pile
X trail
Rewritten sentences: I carted away the pile of weeds. We opened the trail the next day.
Sentences will vary.

Lesson 5
Page 88
Numbered reasons in paragraph: (1) Our equipment is left over from last year (2) most of the few pieces we have are damaged (3) Having better playground equipment will help us to get more exercise at recess.

Page 89
Reasons and letters will vary.

Lesson 6
Page 91
heading
inside address
greeting
body
closing
signature
Dear Mr. Martinsen:
Cordially,

Lesson 7
Page 92
Responses will vary.

Page 93
Entries in chart will vary.

Page 94
Business letter drafts will vary.

Page 96
Revisions will vary.

Answer Key

Chapter 7

Lesson 1

Page 98
Responses will vary.

Lesson 2

Page 99
Cause: The lever moves. Effect: The track moves.
Cause: The track moves. Effect: The figures appear to dance.

Page 100
Cause: Jason put an ad in the paper. Effect: He got many responses.
Cause: He got many responses. Effect: He didn't have time to do his schoolwork.
Cause: Jason didn't do his schoolwork. Effect: He got in trouble.
Responses will vary.

Lesson 3

Page 101
Circled words: so, As a result, Because, As a result

Page 102
Responses will vary.

Lesson 4

Page 103
Circled verbs and past tense form:
slow—slowed
watch—watched
cover—covered
howl—howled
close—closed
wonder—wondered

Page 104
Circled verbs and past tense form:
drives—drove
begins—began

drinks—drank
eats—ate
takes—took
runs—ran
Sentences will vary.

Lesson 5

Page 106
Responses will vary.

Lesson 6

Page 108
Directions will vary.

Page 109
Responses will vary.

Page 110
Entries in chart will vary.

Page 111
Instructions will vary.

Page 113
Revisions will vary.

Page 115
Final instructions will vary.

Answer Key

Chapter 8

Lesson 1

Page 118
Circled transition words in report on page
    116: As a result, so, but
Responses will vary.

Lesson 2

Page 120
Paragraphs will vary.

Lesson 3

Page 121
Responses and time lines will vary.

Page 122
Entries in chart will vary.

Page 123
Biographies will vary.

Page 125
Revisions will vary.

Page 127
Final biographies will vary.